Four Tragedies of Shakespeare

Charles Lamb & Mary Lamb

Level 4
(2000-word)

Adapted by Miki Terasawa

IBC パブリッシング

はじめに

　ラダーシリーズは、「はしご（ladder）」を使って一歩一歩上を目指すように、学習者の実力に合わせ、無理なくステップアップできるよう開発された英文リーダーのシリーズです。

　リーディング力をつけるためには、繰り返したくさん読むこと、いわゆる「多読」がもっとも効果的な学習法であると言われています。多読では、「1. 速く 2. 訳さず英語のまま 3. なるべく辞書を使わず」に読むことが大切です。スピードを計るなど、速く読むよう心がけましょう（たとえばTOEIC®テストの音声スピードはおよそ1分間に150語です）。そして1語ずつ訳すのではなく、英語を英語のまま理解するくせをつけるようにします。こうして読み続けるうちに語感がついてきて、だんだんと英語が理解できるようになるのです。まずは、ラダーシリーズの中からあなたのレベルに合った本を選び、少しずつ英文に慣れ親しんでください。たくさんの本を手にとるうちに、英文書がすらすら読めるようになってくるはずです。

《本シリーズの特徴》
- 中学校レベルから中級者レベルまで5段階に分かれています。自分に合ったレベルからスタートしてください。
- クラシックから現代文学、ノンフィクション、ビジネスと幅広いジャンルを扱っています。あなたの興味に合わせてタイトルを選べます。
- 巻末のワードリストで、いつでもどこでも単語の意味を確認できます。レベル1、2では、文中の全ての単語が、レベル3以上は中学校レベル外の単語が掲載されています。
- カバーにヘッドホーンマークのついているタイトルは、オーディオ・サポートがあります。ウェブから購入／ダウンロードし、リスニング教材としても併用できます。

《使用語彙について》

レベル1：中学校で学習する単語約1000語

レベル2：レベル1の単語＋使用頻度の高い単語約300語

レベル3：レベル1の単語＋使用頻度の高い単語約600語

レベル4：レベル1の単語＋使用頻度の高い単語約1000語

レベル5：語彙制限なし

Contents

Hamlet ... 1

Othello ... 31

King Lear ... 55

Macbeth ... 75

Word List ... 96

Hamlet

【キーワード】

☐ cruel ☐ deed ☐ depressed
☐ duel ☐ funeral ☐ ghost
☐ grave ☐ mureder ☐ pirates
☐ widow

【あらすじ】

　デンマークの王子ハムレットは、父王が亡くなってすぐに母が叔父と再婚したことに腹を立てていた。叔父は王位篡奪のために父を暗殺したのではないかと疑ってもいた。そんなある日、ハムレットは城に現れた父の亡霊と会う。亡霊は、自分を殺した敵・叔父クローディアスに復讐して欲しいという。

【主な登場人物】

Hamlet ハムレット　デンマークの王。予期せず急逝する。

Gertrude ガートルード　デンマークの王妃。未亡人になるが、すぐに先王の実弟と再婚する。

Hamlet ハムレット　父王と同名の王子。母の再婚を憎み、再婚相手の叔父が父を暗殺したのではないかと疑っている。

Horatio ホレイシオ　ハムレット王子が深く信頼している親友。

Claudius クローディアス　先王の実弟。未亡人となった王妃と結婚し、王位を継ぐ。

Polonius ポローニアス　宰相。先王時代からのご意見番。

Ophelia オフィーリア　宰相ポローニアスの娘。ハムレット王子の恋人。

Laertes レアーティーズ　オフィーリアの兄。

ACT ONE

Once in the country of Denmark there lived a noble king named Hamlet. His queen was named Gertrude. They had a grown son, also named Hamlet, who was as noble and good as his father.

But King Hamlet died suddenly and unexpectedly, leaving Queen Gertrude a widow. Less than two months later, Queen Gertrude married her dead husband's brother, Claudius.

Many people were shocked by this marriage. They thought it was wrong that Queen Gertrude had remarried so quickly. They thought it was also wrong and even unnatural that the queen had married her husband's own brother.

Also, Claudius was neither wise nor good, as the dead King Hamlet had been. Some people wondered if Claudius had secretly killed his brother to become king. They thought that perhaps Claudius wanted to take the place of the rightful king, young Prince Hamlet, the son of the dead king.

Prince Hamlet was extremely shocked by his mother's marriage to his uncle Claudius. Hamlet had loved his father very much. He had a strong sense of honor, and his mother's marriage seemed very wrong to him. Hamlet felt great sadness about his father's death. He also felt terrible shame about his mother's new marriage.

The young prince Hamlet was filled with sadness. He never laughed any more. He was never happy anymore. Nothing he did gave him pleasure. He could find no relief in books or sport or other activities. To Hamlet, the world suddenly seemed to be a sad and worthless place. It was like a garden filled with weeds where no flowers could grow.

Hamlet was angry that his uncle Claudius was now king. But to this proud and honorable young prince, that was not the worst thing. What made Hamlet most sad was his mother's behavior. He was shocked that Gertrude was so forgetful of her dead husband's memory. The dead King Hamlet had been so noble, kind, and loving—the best of all husbands. And in times past, Queen Gertrude had seemed like such a loving and obedient wife to him.

But now, less than two months after the king's death, she had married again to the king's own brother! To marry Hamlet's uncle seemed like a very improper and even unlawful thing.

The speed of the marriage made it seem even less proper to Hamlet. And Claudius was a man of little honor and nobility. He seemed so unkingly compared to the dead King Hamlet. These thoughts about his mother and her new husband made Hamlet very depressed and sad.

* * * *

His mother Queen Gertrude and her new husband King Claudius tried hard to cheer Prince Hamlet and make him happy again. But nothing worked. Hamlet remained sad and depressed. He refused to wear any color except black, to honor the memory of his dead father. He even wore black on his mother's wedding day to Claudius. He would not participate in any of the celebrations of that wedding day, either. Everything related to his mother's new marriage seemed shameful and disgraceful to Hamlet.

Instead, Hamlet spent all of his time wondering about his father's sudden death. It had been unexpected and most mysterious. According to Claudius, King Hamlet had been lying asleep in the garden and had been bitten by a snake. The snake's bite had killed the king, Claudius said.

But young Hamlet did not believe what Claudius said. In fact, Hamlet often wondered if Claudius had killed the king, murdering him in order to gain the throne and marry Gertrude.

Hamlet could not stop wondering if he was right to suspect that Claudius was his father's murderer. He also wondered about his mother Gertrude. Had she known about Claudius's plan to kill King Hamlet? Was she guilty of that crime? Was she innocent? These thoughts and these doubts filled Hamlet's mind. He could think of nothing else.

* * * *

Then one day Hamlet heard a strange story from the soldiers who guarded the castle at night. The soldiers said that they had seen a ghost. The ghost had looked exactly like the dead King Hamlet. The ghost's face and figure resembled him in every way. It even wore the same suit of armor that the dead king had always worn.

According to the soldiers, this ghost had appeared at midnight for the past two or three nights. Hamlet's best friend, Horatio, had seen the ghost, as well. The ghost looked pale and sad, Horatio said. It had a beard of dark and silver hair, just like the dead King Hamlet had once had. When the soldiers tried to speak to the ghost, it looked at them but did not answer. Then the ghost disappeared, as the night ended and the light of morning came.

The young Prince Hamlet was amazed by this strange and mysterious story. He agreed with the soldiers and Horatio that the ghost must have been his dead father the king. On the very next night, Prince Hamlet decided to go with the soldiers and try to see the ghost for himself. Hamlet thought that the ghost might have something important to tell him. He hoped that the ghost would speak to him, since he was the dead king's beloved son.

* * * *

Prince Hamlet waited impatiently for night to come. At last, when it was almost midnight, he climbed up to the roof of the castle. Hamlet was accompanied by Horatio and one of the soldiers, Marcellus. The three men stood on the roof in the cold, dark night. They waited to see if the ghost would come. They waited for a long while. Then suddenly they saw the ghostly figure of a man appear.

At the sight of his father's spirit, Prince Hamlet was surprised and afraid. He called on the angels to defend them, since they could not tell if the ghost was good or bad. Perhaps it was an evil spirit! Perhaps it was the devil in disguise!

But slowly Hamlet became brave again. The ghost looked very much like Hamlet's father, and its face was sad. It seemed to want to speak with him.

Hamlet called to the ghost, calling it by his father's name, "Hamlet! King! Father!" He begged the ghost to tell him why it had left its grave and come to visit the earth again. "What can we do to give peace to your spirit?" Hamlet asked.

The ghost lifted its hand and beckoned to Hamlet. It seemed to want him to come closer and to go to a private place where they could be alone. Horatio and Marcellus were afraid. They wanted to stop Hamlet from following the ghost. They were worried that the ghost might lead Hamlet to his death, or perhaps it would make him go crazy.

But Hamlet was determined to follow the ghost. He cared so little for his life that he did not fear losing it. Pushing Horatio and Marcellus away, Hamlet quickly followed the ghost.

When the ghost and Hamlet were alone together, the ghost began to speak. "I am the ghost of your father, the dead King Hamlet," the ghost said to the prince. "I was cruelly and secretly murdered by my brother, your uncle Claudius."

Then the ghost explained to Hamlet how he had been murdered. "I was sleeping in the garden one afternoon. Then my evil brother Claudius came quietly to my side. As I slept, he poured a deadly poison in my ear. I was killed instantly. Thus I lost my kingdom, my queen, and my life. If you ever loved your dear father, Hamlet, you will revenge my murder. Take revenge on your uncle Claudius."

The ghost continued to speak. "But do not take any revenge on your mother, Queen Gertrude. It is true that she has done wrong by remarrying. But leave her to the judgment of Heaven and to the bitterness of her own soul."

Hamlet was shocked and shaken by what the ghost said. He promised to do as the ghost requested. Then the ghost disappeared, leaving the prince alone.

Immediately Hamlet made a promise to himself: "I will forget everything else I ever knew or learned. The only thing that matters to me now is what the ghost said. I will do what the ghost requested. I will take revenge upon Claudius."

Then Prince Hamlet returned to Horatio and Marcellus. He made them promise to keep the events of the night secret. "You must tell no one what we saw!" Hamlet said. Both men promised to keep the secret.

Later, Hamlet told Horatio exactly what the ghost had said. Since Horatio was Hamlet's best friend, Hamlet knew that he would not tell anyone else.

ACT TWO

Seeing his dead father's ghost was a terrifying experience for Hamlet. Even before that, his mind had been weak and depressed. But now, after seeing the ghost, Hamlet's mind was on the edge of madness. He feared that, because of his strange behavior, his uncle Claudius might suspect something. So Hamlet decided that he would pretend to be completely and truly mad. Then, Hamlet thought, Claudius would believe that he was no threat at all.

From that time on, Hamlet began to talk and dress and act strangely. His pretend madness was so well done that his mother Queen Gertrude and the new King Claudius believed that it was real. They thought that poor Prince Hamlet was truly mad. But they thought that love was the reason behind the prince's madness.

It was true that Hamlet had once been in love. Before the death of the old King, he had been in love with a beautiful girl named Ophelia. She was the daughter of Polonius, the king's chief counselor. Hamlet had sent Ophelia gifts and told her that he loved her. Ophelia had believed in Hamlet's love and been happy.

But now, in his depression and seeming madness, Hamlet often ignored Ophelia. He sometimes treated her unkindly and rudely. But Ophelia did not become angry. She only felt sorry for Hamlet. She wished that he would become happy again.

At times, Hamlet felt guilty about treating Ophelia so badly. In his heart, he still loved her. So he wrote her a letter to show his love. "Doubt that the stars are fire, doubt that the sun does move, doubt truth to be a liar, but never to doubt that I love," he wrote to her.

Being a good daughter, Ophelia showed this letter to her father Polonius. Polonius then showed the letter to the King and Queen. That was why the King and Queen thought that the cause of Hamlet's madness was love. Queen Gertrude hoped that Hamlet would someday marry Ophelia, and then his madness would disappear.

But Hamlet's seeming madness could not be so easily cured. The real cause was his father's murder and Hamlet's promise to the ghost. Hamlet was always thinking of the ghost's demand for revenge. He was never at peace. But he could not think of a plan to accomplish this revenge. King Claudius was always surrounded by his guards, or he was accompanied by Queen Gertrude.

In addition, Hamlet was such an honorable prince that he sometimes struggled with the idea of killing at all. Finally, Hamlet sometimes doubted the ghost. He wondered if the ghost had truly spoken the truth. What if the ghost was not his father?

Perhaps the ghost had been the devil in disguise, speaking lies to get Hamlet to commit a terrible crime against his uncle. Therefore Hamlet decided that he needed more proof. He would find another way to determine if his uncle Claudius was innocent or guilty.

* * * *

Around this same time, a group of actors came to the palace. In earlier, happier days, Hamlet had loved to watch these actors perform. Hamlet greeted the actors and welcomed them gladly. He asked them to perform one of his favorite scenes. The scene described the death of old Priam, the King of Troy, and the grief of Hecuba, his queen. The actors performed the scene excellently. They described the cruel murder of the old king and the grief of the old queen. They acted it so well that everyone who watched began to cry. Even the actors cried.

The wonderful acting made Hamlet think. He remembered hearing a story about a murderer who watched a play about a murder just like the one he had committed. Seeing the murder on stage made the murderer so upset that he confessed to his crime.

ACT THREE

So Hamlet decided that he would ask the actors to perform a play that showed a murder just like his father's. If Claudius watched it and got upset, then Hamlet would know that he had committed the murder.

The story of the play was of the murder of a Viennese duke. The duke's name was Gonzago, and his wife's name was Baptista. The murderer was named Lucianus, and he was part of the duke's family. The play showed how the evil Lucianus poisoned Duke Gonzago as he lay sleeping in his garden. Then Lucianus became the duke and took over Gonzago's house and lands. Soon afterwards, Lucianus gained the love of the widowed Baptista and then quickly married her.

On the night that the play was to be performed, King Claudius and Queen Gertrude were watching. Hamlet sat near the king, in order to see how he reacted to the story of the murder.

The play began with a conversation between

Gonzago and his wife Baptista. She said that she loved Gonzago very much. She promised that she would never marry another man. Baptista also said that only evil women who kill their first husbands would ever marry a second time.

Hearing these words, King Claudius and Queen Gertrude both turned pale. Hamlet saw this and continued to watch his uncle and his mother carefully. The play continued with the murder of Gonzago in the garden. The murder of Gonzago was exactly like the murder of King Hamlet, and Claudius was frightened by the similarity. Hamlet watched as King Claudius jumped up from his chair and demanded that the play be stopped.

Then Claudius hurried out of the room, claiming that he felt sick. The actors stopped, and the play quickly came to an end.

* * * *

Now Hamlet was satisfied, and he reached a decision. "I am sure," he said to his friend Horatio, "that the ghost spoke the truth. My uncle, King Claudius, acted like a guilty man when he saw the murder of Gonzago. I am certain that Claudius killed my dear father, King Hamlet. Now I am ready to take revenge for my father's death."

But as soon as Hamlet had spoken these words, he received an important message. His mother, Queen Gertrude, had called him to her room. The queen was very upset and angry, and she wanted to speak with him immediately.

King Claudius had asked Gertrude to speak with Hamlet. Claudius told Gertrude, "You must tell Hamlet how much he has displeased and angered us." But Claudius also wanted to know exactly what Hamlet said during this meeting. So Claudius ordered Polonius, his old advisor, to hide behind a curtain and listen to the conversation. Polonius was happy to do this work of spying for the king.

* * * *

When Hamlet came to his mother's room, she began to criticize him. "You have greatly offended your father, Hamlet," Queen Gertrude said. (When she said "father," she was talking about King Claudius, Hamlet's uncle. Gertrude considered Claudius to be Hamlet's father because he was married to her, Hamlet's mother.)

Gertrude's words angered Hamlet. He was furious that she had called Claudius his "father." So he replied to Gertrude very sharply: "Mother, you have greatly offended *my* father."

The queen said that Hamlet was talking nonsense. "It is no more than your question deserved," replied Hamlet.

"Have you forgotten to whom you are speaking?" Queen Gertrude asked sternly.

"Alas!" replied Hamlet, "I wish I could forget. You are the queen. You are your husband's brother's wife, and you are my mother. I wish you were not what you are."

"Then if you show me so little respect," said Queen Gertrude, "I will have you speak to the King." She prepared to leave the room to go call the King.

But Hamlet would not let her go. Now that he was alone with his mother, he was determined to try to show her how wicked she had been. He grabbed her arm. He forced her to sit down.

Gertrude was frightened by Hamlet's serious face and by his seeming madness. She cried out in fear.

Then suddenly another voice was heard. It came from behind the curtains of the room, crying, "Help, help the Queen!"

When Hamlet heard the voice, he thought it was the king hiding behind the curtain. Angrily he took out his sword and stabbed at the place where the voice came from.

The voice fell silent, and Hamlet dragged a body from behind the curtains. But it was not the king; it was old Polonius, who had been hiding and spying on their conversation.

"Oh, me!" exclaimed the queen. "What a rash and bloody deed have you done!"

"A bloody deed, mother," replied Hamlet. "But it is not so bad as yours. You killed a king and married his brother."

Hamlet had gone too far to stop now. He decided to speak honestly and plainly to his mother. He wanted to show her that her actions had been very wrong.

"How could you forget the dead king, my father?" Hamlet asked Gertrude. "He was an excellent husband and king. How could you, so soon after his death, marry his brother and suspected murderer? The heavens are ashamed of you, Mother. All marriage promises seem empty and false because of your actions. Religion seems like a joke."

Then Hamlet showed Gertrude two pictures. The

first showed the dead King Hamlet, and the second picture showed the new King Claudius.

"Look at the differences between these pictures!" Hamlet cried. "Look at my father. See how like a god he looked. He had the curls of Apollo, the forehead of Jupiter, the eye of Mars, and a posture like Mercury. This kingly man had been your husband."

Then Hamlet pointed to the second picture, of King Claudius. "Now look your new husband, Mother. He has no goodness, no wisdom, no kindness, no greatness. And he was the one who killed my father."

Queen Gertrude felt great shame. Suddenly she was forced to look at her own heart and soul. She saw that they were black.

Then Hamlet asked her, "How can you continue to live with this man, and be his wife? He murdered your first husband and stole the crown and kingdom from him."

But just then, Hamlet saw the ghost of his father enter the room. Suddenly full of fear, Hamlet asked the ghost what it wanted. The ghost reminded him of his promise: revenge King Hamlet's death, but not to harm Queen Gertrude.

"Speak gently to your mother," the ghost told

Hamlet. "Otherwise, the grief and fear will kill her." Then the ghost of old King Hamlet disappeared again.

Meanwhile, Queen Gertrude watched Hamlet but could not see the ghost. She only saw her son talking to no one, and she feared that he was very mad.

But Hamlet told her, "I am not mad. My father's ghost came back to earth because of your wrongdoing, not my madness. Feel my heart beat, Mother. It beats calmly, not like a madman's."

Then Hamlet begged Gertrude to confess herself to Heaven. He told her to ask forgiveness for her deeds. He told her to avoid the king and no longer act as his wife. That way, Hamlet explained, Gertrude would be acting like a true mother to him again. Shocked and upset, Gertrude promised to do as Hamlet wished.

And now Hamlet looked carefully at the man whom he had killed. He realized that it was Polonius, the father of Ophelia. Hamlet still loved Ophelia, and he felt terrible that he had killed her father. He knew that it would hurt Ophelia when she found out that Polonius was dead.

ACT FOUR

The death of Polonius gave King Claudius a reason to send Hamlet out of the kingdom. He secretly wanted to put Hamlet to death because he thought that he was dangerous.

But Claudius knew that Queen Gertrude loved Hamlet and would never allow him to be killed. Claudius also knew that Hamlet was very popular with the people of Denmark. They would be angry if he were killed.

So this evil king used Polonius's death to get Hamlet out of Denmark. He put Hamlet on a ship that was sailing to England. He sent two servants with Hamlet, too. These servants were given letters for the English rulers. The letters commanded that Hamlet be killed as soon as he arrived in England.

* * * *

But Hamlet suspected that King Claudius was trying to kill him. So, one night during the sea voyage, while the servants were sleeping, Hamlet found the letters and opened them. He erased his name from the letters and put the servants' names in its place. Then he quickly closed and sealed the letters again.

* * * *

Soon afterwards, Hamlet's ship was attacked by pirates. A terrible battle began. Hamlet fought bravely and even fought his way onto the pirates' ship. But then his own ship sailed away toward England, leaving Hamlet with the pirates. (The two servants of King Claudius were still aboard the ship. They sailed to England with the letters that would lead to their own deaths.)

* * * *

Meanwhile, the pirates were gracious to Hamlet. They realized that he was the prince of Denmark. They hoped that Hamlet would treat them well in the future, if they treated him kindly now. So the pirates sailed with Hamlet and took him to the first port they reached in Denmark. When they arrived in Denmark, they allowed Hamlet to leave the ship.

Once Hamlet arrived in Denmark, he wrote a letter to King Claudius. In the letter, Hamlet told the king about the strange adventure that had brought him back to his own country. Hamlet also told the king that he would return to the court the next day.

ACT FIVE

But when Hamlet arrived back at the palace, he saw a sad and tragic event. This event was the funeral of the young and beautiful Ophelia, the girl whom Hamlet had once loved. Ophelia had begun to lose her mind and go mad after her father Polonius's shocking and unexpected death. The fact that Polonius had been killed by Hamlet, the man she loved, was too much for poor Ophelia. Slowly, her behavior and her speech became strange and confused. She would walk around, giving flowers away to the ladies of the court. She said that these flowers were for her father's funeral. She also sang sad songs about love and death. Sometimes she sang songs that seemed to have no meaning at all. She often seemed as if she had lost her memory entirely.

Her death had been an accident. There was a willow which grew over a brook. Its branches and leaves hung over the water. One day Ophelia came to this brook. She brought chains of flowers and weeds that she had made. She climbed up into the willow tree to hang her flowers upon it.

But suddenly the branch broke, and Ophelia fell into the water below. For a while, she floated in the water. As she floated, she sang bits of strange songs. She did not seem to realize that she was in danger. But finally her clothes became soaked with water, and they pulled her down into the stream, where she quickly died.

Ophelia's brother Laertes had organized the funeral. All the court was there, including King Claudius and Queen Gertrude. At this moment, Hamlet arrived at the funeral. At first, Hamlet did not realize whose funeral it was. He stood quietly and watched for a while. He saw the flowers that were being thrown on Ophelia's grave.

Then Hamlet saw his mother, Queen Gertrude, throw flowers, too. He heard her say, "Sweets to the sweet! I had hoped to decorate your bridal bed, not throw flowers on your grave. You should have been the wife of my Hamlet." Hearing those words, Hamlet realized that Ophelia had died.

Then Ophelia's brother Laertes spoke. "May flowers grow from her grave," he said. Filled with sadness, Laertes then jumped into Ophelia's open grave. He called to the people to fill the grave and cover him with dirt, because he wanted to be buried with his dear sister.

Watching Laertes, Hamlet remembered how much he had loved Ophelia himself. "I loved Ophelia more than forty thousand brothers," Hamlet cried. Then he threw himself into the grave, too.

Once Laertes saw Hamlet, he quickly recognized him. He was very angry to see him there. Laertes blamed Hamlet for the death of Ophelia. He also blamed Hamlet for his father Polonius's death.

Laertes grabbed Hamlet by the throat, and the two men began to fight. Finally, the other people of the court pulled them apart. The fight ended.

Later, after the funeral, Hamlet apologized to Laertes. He said that he had been so upset by Ophelia's death that he could not stop himself from jumping into her grave. Laertes seemed to accept Hamlet's apology.

* * * *

But the evil King Claudius found a way to use Laertes's grief and anger for his own purposes. Claudius sent Laertes to challenge Hamlet to a friendly duel. (Both young men were considered to be excellent sword-fighters.) It was supposed to be an act of peace and friendship, Laertes told Hamlet. But secretly, Claudius had Laertes put poison on the tip of his sword. The poison was a deadly one, and it would kill anyone who was wounded by the sword. Hamlet did not suspect Laertes of any wrongdoing, and he did not look carefully at the swords.

Then the duel began. All of the court watched with great enjoyment. At first, Laertes let Hamlet win a few points during the duel. The evil king pretended to cheer for Hamlet and hope for his victory. But then Laertes decided to act. He charged forward and wounded Hamlet with the poisoned sword.

Hamlet knew that he had been wounded, although he did not realize that the sword was poisoned. Angry and determined to continue fighting, Hamlet accidentally grabbed Laertes's sword. Then he wounded Laertes with the deadly sword, poisoning him, too.

At that moment, Queen Gertrude gave a terrible cry. "I have been poisoned!" she cried. She had accidentally drunk out of a cup that Claudius had poisoned. The poison had been meant for Hamlet, in case Hamlet had escaped from Laertes's duel unharmed. The queen quickly died.

Hamlet suspected that someone was behind this evil deed. He decided to find out who it was. He ordered all the doors to be closed. "Let no one leave the room!" he cried.

Then the wounded Laertes spoke. He told Hamlet that he was the traitor. Knowing that he was dying, Laertes told Hamlet everything. He explained how the sword was poisoned and how both he and Hamlet would die from their wounds. "You have less than half an hour to live," Laertes told Hamlet. "No medicine can cure you."

With his final breaths, Laertes asked Hamlet for his forgiveness. He also told Hamlet that King Claudius was to blame.

Hamlet felt himself growing weak from the poison. With the last of his strength, he suddenly turned to his evil uncle Claudius. He quickly thrust the poisoned sword into Claudius's heart. Claudius fell down dead. At last, Hamlet had kept his promise to his father's ghost. He had revenged his father's murder.

Then Hamlet felt the end of his life drawing near. He turned to his best friend Horatio, who had seen everything. With his dying breath, Hamlet asked Horatio to stay alive for his sake and to tell his story to the world. (At first, Horatio had wanted to kill himself, to join Hamlet in death.)

Horatio agreed to Hamlet's request. He promised to continue living to tell the truth of Hamlet's tragedy. Finally at peace, Prince Hamlet died.

With many tears, Horatio and the court prayed for the spirit of the dead prince to be among the angels in Heaven. Hamlet's death was a cause of great sadness throughout Denmark. He had been a noble and good prince who was loved by all. If he had lived, he would have been a great and royal king of Denmark.

Othello

【キーワード】

☐deceive　　☐general　　☐jealous
☐lieutenant　☐Moor　　　☐noble
☐proof　　　☐Turks

【あらすじ】

ヴェニスの黒人将軍オセローは、数々の障害を乗り越えて愛するデズデモーナと結婚した。愛妻とともに対トルコ戦争の前線であるサイプラス島へ赴任する。オセローが夫妻の共通の友人でもある部下のキャシオを副官に任命すると、その人事がイアーゴーという男の嫉妬と怒りに火をつけた。イアーゴーはキャシオとオセロー、デズデモーナを破滅に追いやるべく画策しはじめる。

【主な登場人物】

Brabantio ブラバンショー　ヴェニスの裕福な元老院議員。デズデモーナの父。

Desdemona デズデモーナ　美しく心優しい、ブラバンショーの一人娘。オセローの妻となる。

Othello オセロー　黒い肌の外国人でありながらヴェニスの将軍となった勇敢な軍人。

Michael Cassio マイケル・キャシオ　若くハンサムなイタリア人の貴族。上司のオセローに目をかけられている。

Iago イアーゴー　オセローの部下で、キャシオの先輩。キャシオとオセローに反感を持ち、陰謀を企てる。

Emilia エミリア　イアーゴーの妻で、デズデモーナの侍女。

ACT ONE

In the Italian city of Venice, there was once a rich man named Brabantio. Brabantio was a senator and a leader of Venice. He had a beautiful and gentle daughter, Desdemona.

Many noble Venetian men wanted to marry Desdemona. But she was not interested in any of these men. Instead, she fell in love with a Moor named Othello. Othello was a friend of Brabantio and was often invited to his house.

It was understandable why Desdemona fell in love with Othello. Although he was black and not Italian, the Moor had many noble qualities. He was a soldier, and a very brave one. After fighting bravely in many wars against the Turks and winning many battles, Othello had become a Venetian general. He was greatly respected and trusted by the leaders of Venice.

Othello had traveled to many places and had done many things in his life. Desdemona was fascinated by his exciting stories of his adventures. Othello told her about the wars he had fought in. He told her about the many dangers he had escaped. He described the many strange and beautiful foreign places he had seen.

Othello also told Desdemona the story of his life. Hearing the story, Desdemona fell in love with Othello's courage, strength, wisdom, and noble ways. Then Othello told her that he loved her, too. Soon Desdemona secretly agreed to marry him.

* * * *

Unfortunately, Desdemona's father Brabantio did not approve of her marriage. Although Othello was brave and a respected general, Brabantio did not want Desdemona to marry a black-skinned Moor. He had expected that his daughter would marry a noble Venetian man instead.

When Brabantio discovered the secret marriage, he was shocked and angry. He accused Othello of using evil magic to trick Desdemona into marrying him.

But at this same time, the leaders of Venice needed Othello's help as a general. The Turks, who were the enemies of Venice, were planning a war. The Turks were sending warships to attack the island of Cyprus, which was controlled by the Venetians. The leaders of Venice wanted Othello to protect Cyprus.

So Othello was called before the Venetian leaders for two different reasons. First, the leaders wanted him to protect Cyprus from the Turks. Second, Othello had to explain and defend his marriage to Desdemona.

* * * *

When Othello met the Venetian leaders, he spoke honestly about his love for Desdemona. Othello explained how he had told Desdemona the story of his life. He explained how she had fallen in love with him. He said that he loved Desdemona's gentle nature, beauty, and kindness.

Hearing Othello's words, the Venetian leaders agreed that he had not used evil magic to win Desdemona's heart. He had acted nobly and honorably, they said.

Othello's words were supported by Desdemona, too. She spoke to the Venetian leaders and explained why she had married Othello. She explained that she had a duty to her father for giving her life and an education.

However, she had an even greater duty to her new husband, whom she loved. "Othello is a good and noble man," Desdemona told the Venetian leaders. "He won my heart by noble means."

After Brabantio heard Othello and Desdemona speak, he was forced to agree. He called Othello to him. Sadly he said, "I give you my daughter, but I do it without happiness. No good can come of this marriage, I think. Truly, I am glad that I have no other children," Brabantio continued. "Desdemona betrayed my trust. If I had any other children, I would no longer trust them, either."

ACT TWO

Then Othello and Desdemona left Venice together as man and wife. They sailed to the island of Cyprus. There, Othello would be the Venetian general, defending the island against the Turks. Desdemona was glad to travel with her new husband. She was not afraid of the dangers of war. She wanted only to be with her beloved Othello.

When Othello and Desdemona arrived in Cyprus, they received very good news. A sudden storm had come upon the sea. The storm had destroyed the Turkish warships. The island of Cyprus was safe, at least for the present time.

But now Othello and Desdemona were about to face a different kind of evil. Othello's enemies were plotting, and their actions would be more deadly than the Turks. In fact, their actions would be deadly to both Othello and his new wife.

* * * *

Many Venetian officers had come to Cyprus with Othello. One of them was a young Italian nobleman named Michael Cassio. This young man was Othello's best friend and favorite among all of the officers. Cassio was a young soldier of many excellent qualities. He was handsome, happy, intelligent, and had a pleasing manner. He was very popular with women. In fact, Cassio was exactly the kind of young man who might make a husband jealous, especially a husband like Othello with a beautiful wife.

However, Othello was as free from jealousy as he was noble. During his courtship of Desdemona in Venice, Othello had even trusted Cassio as a messenger to Desdemona. As Othello's friend, Cassio had often talked to Desdemona about Othello's many virtues.

Therefore it was no surprise that the gentle Desdemona loved and trusted Cassio. She considered him a friend because he was Othello's dear friend. In Cyprus, Cassio came often to Othello and Desdemona's home. He talked and laughed freely with both of them.

Recently, Othello had promoted Cassio to be his lieutenant. This was a very important position, and it showed to the world how much Othello liked and trusted Cassio.

But this promotion was the cause of some jealousy among other soldiers. In particular, Cassio's promotion angered another soldier named Iago. Iago was older and had served in the army longer than Cassio. Iago thought that he should have gotten the position of lieutenant instead.

Iago had always hated Cassio, and now he began to hate Othello as well, for favoring Cassio. In his jealousy, Iago also thought that Othello was too fond of his own wife Emilia. This idea was completely untrue, for Othello only loved Desdemona. But this idea stuck in the brain of the jealous and angry Iago.

And so, full of rage and evil ideas, Iago began to plot a terrible revenge. He hoped that his revenge would lead Cassio, Othello, and Desdemona all together into tragedy and ruin.

Iago was a very clever man. He had studied human nature carefully. He knew that jealousy could be a powerful weapon. If he could succeed in making Othello jealous of Cassio, Iago thought, it would be a perfect revenge. In fact, it might end in the death of Cassio or Othello, or both.

* * * *

After Othello and Desdemona arrived in Cyprus, there were many celebrations. The storm had destroyed the Turkish warships, and everyone was happy. Great feasts were held, and much wine was drunk. Everyone celebrated the arrival of the Moor Othello and his new lady, the fair Desdemona.

As lieutenant, Cassio was responsible for the guard that night. Othello had ordered Cassio to keep the soldiers from drinking too much. He did not want the people of Cyprus to be displeased with his soldiers.

That same night Iago decided to put his plans for revenge into motion. He tricked Cassio into drinking too much. "We must drink to the health of the noble Othello," Iago said to Cassio. "We must drink to the health of his fair Desdemona!"

Cassio tried to resist, but he was tricked by Iago's evil plan. Cassio drank many cups of wine, while Iago pretended to drink, too.

Once Cassio was drunk, Iago started a fight between Cassio and another soldier. Soon the fight turned into a large brawl of many soldiers. Then Iago rang the alarm-bell of the castle. The sound of the bell awakened Othello, who hurried outside. He sternly asked Cassio what had happened.

Poor Cassio had now recovered from the wine he had drunk. But his mind was still cloudy, and he had forgotten exactly what had happened earlier in the evening. Cassio was too much ashamed to reply to Othello.

Then Othello asked Iago what had happened. At first, Iago pretended that he did not want to blame Cassio. He acted as if he were Cassio's good friend. But finally he told Othello about Cassio's drinking—while not mentioning his own actions. Speaking cleverly, Iago made Cassio look very irresponsible.

When Othello heard Iago's story, he was very disappointed with Cassio. As punishment, Othello took away Cassio's position as lieutenant.

In this way, Iago achieved the first part of his revenge. Cassio had lost Othello's favor. But Iago was not finished with his evil plans for revenge.

Cassio was very sad. "I was such a fool!" he said to Iago. "What should I do? I made a mistake, but I cannot ask Othello to make me lieutenant again."

Iago listened to Cassio and pretended to be a sympathetic friend. "I will give you some good advice," he said. Iago told Cassio to ask for Desdemona's help. "The Lady Desdemona can help you," Iago said. "Othello loves her. If Desdemona asks Othello to forgive you, as a favor to her, then Othello will do it. Desdemona is a kind and helpful lady. As your friend, she will gladly plead your case with her husband."

Cassio, who now considered Iago his good friend, thanked him. He did as Iago advised him. Cassio went to Desdemona immediately. He asked for her help with Othello. "If you plead my case to Othello, he will forgive me," Cassio said.

ACT THREE

Full of pity for Cassio, the kind Desdemona quickly agreed to help him. Immediately, Desdemona began to talk to Othello about Cassio. Every day she pleaded with her husband on Cassio's behalf. She asked so prettily and earnestly that Othello could not easily say no.

However, Othello was still very angry with Cassio. "Cassio behaved very badly," Othello said to his wife. "You must understand that I cannot quickly forgive him."

But Desdemona continued to plead for Cassio. "My lord, Cassio is your good friend. He is an honorable man. When you wanted to marry me, you often sent Cassio to plead your case. Do you not remember? Can you not forgive him?"

At last, Othello agreed to forgive Cassio. "I promise to forgive Cassio. But be patient," he told Desdemona. "I will forgive him at the right time."

* * * *

The next day, Othello and Iago entered Desdemona's room just as Cassio was leaving from another door. (Cassio had been asking Desdemona for help with Othello.)

Iago pointed to Cassio as he left the room. Then he quietly said, "I do not like that." At first, Othello did not pay attention to Iago's words. But later he remembered it and asked Iago what he meant.

Iago pretended to be reluctant to answer. He asked Othello if Cassio had known of his love for Desdemona before their marriage. Othello answered yes, and Iago gave him a worried look.

Once more, Othello asked Iago what he was thinking. "Iago, you are a good man. You are an honest man. Tell me what you are thinking! Even if your thoughts are dark, I must know what they are. Tell me!"

"I don't know if I should speak," Iago said. "I would be very sorry if my words caused any trouble. My suspicions may be wrong. It would be terrible if innocent people were harmed. Othello, you must beware of jealousy."

With these evil but clever words, Iago began to

make Othello jealous. Othello spoke again. "My wife is beautiful and kind," he said. "She loves people and is open and friendly. Some husbands might see these as reasons to be jealous of her. But she is an excellent and honorable woman, and in such a woman, these qualities are good. I trust my wife. I must have proof before I think that she is not honest."

Then the clever Iago acted as if he was glad that Othello was slow to become jealous. "I have no proof that the Lady Desdemona is dishonest," Iago said. "I will only say this. I think that you should watch her carefully when Cassio is here. Unlike you, I know what Italian ladies are like. They often do things that they dare not show their husbands. And remember, the Lady Desdemona deceived her father when she married Othello. If she was able to deceive her father, she might deceive her husband, too."

Iago apologized for his words. But Othello asked him to continue to speak. Iago pretended to be reluctant to say anything more, but he did. "Desdemona refused many Italian men as husbands," Iago said to Othello. "Then she married you, a Moor. But now, perhaps she is thinking differently. Perhaps she regrets her choice. She may compare you with the fine, young, light-skinned Italian men of her own country. I think you should not forgive Cassio too soon. Instead, you should see how strongly Desdemona pleads for him. If she continues to plead for Cassio's forgiveness, you might suspect her."

* * * *

Now Iago's revenge on Othello was beginning. The trusting, noble Moor was convinced by Iago's poisonous words. After this conversation, Othello was never at peace. His trust in his wife was destroyed. He was filled with jealousy and suspicion. He could not enjoy his work or his life. His mind was confused with different thoughts.

Sometimes Othello thought that Desdemona was honest. Other times he thought she was dishonest. Sometimes he thought Iago was right. Other times he thought Iago was wrong. Sometimes Othello wished that Iago had never spoken. "I would have been happy never knowing if Desdemona loved Cassio!" he said to himself. "I was happy simply believing that she loved me."

ACT FOUR

Othello's jealousy made him feel almost crazy. Finally, he grabbed Iago by the throat. "Show me proof that Desdemona is dishonest," Othello threatened. "If you have no proof, then I will kill you for speaking such evil words about her."

Iago pretended to be upset. "Then I will give you proof," he said. Then he asked Othello, "Does your wife have a handkerchief with strawberries on it?"

"Yes," said Othello. "I know that handkerchief. It was my first gift to Desdemona."

"I have seen that same handkerchief in Cassio's hands," Iago said.

"If that is true," Othello answered, "then I will have my revenge. I will have Cassio killed within three days. And as for my wife, I will find a way to kill her, too."

To a jealous person, even the smallest thing can seem like proof of wrongdoing. To the jealous Othello, Iago's words about the handkerchief were enough to condemn Desdemona and Cassio to death.

But in truth, Desdemona had never given such a present to Cassio. Loving and loyal to her husband, Desdemona would never have done that. Both Cassio and Desdemona were completely innocent. But the evil Iago had made his wife Emilia (a good, but a weak woman) steal this handkerchief from Desdemona. Then he dropped the handkerchief so that Cassio would find it.

* * * *

The next time Othello was with his wife, he claimed to have a headache. "Please give me your handkerchief to hold against my head." Desdemona gave him the plain white handkerchief that was in her pocket.

"Not this handkerchief," said Othello. "Give me the handkerchief that I gave to you as a gift. Give me the handkerchief with the strawberries on it." But of course Desdemona could not give it to him (since Iago had asked Emilia to secretly take it.)

"That is very bad," said Othello. "That handkerchief was very important. It was given to my mother by an Egyptian woman who was a witch. The witch told my mother that the handkerchief would make my father love her. But if she ever lost the handkerchief, my father would hate her as much as he had once loved her. My mother gave me this handkerchief as she lay dying. She told me to give it to my wife, if I ever married. I did so. You must find it, Desdemona. It is precious and contains powerful magic."

Poor Desdemona was very frightened. She knew that the handkerchief had disappeared, although she did not know where it had gone. She was afraid that she had lost both the handkerchief and Othello's love.

To distract Othello, she tried to speak cheerfully. She told Othello that all his talk about the handkerchief was only to keep her from talking about Cassio.

Desdemona began to praise Cassio (as Iago had predicted). Once again, she asked Othello to forgive him. But the jealous Othello could not bear to hear his wife talk about Cassio. He ran from the room, leaving Desdemona very confused. Although she did not understand why, she began to think that her husband was jealous.

Sad and confused, Desdemona began to accuse herself. She thought that she must have displeased her husband in some way. Or perhaps he had gotten bad news from Venice. In any case, she criticized herself: "Men are not gods. It is wrong for women to expect them to always be sweet-tempered. I must not judge him unkindly."

* * * *

When Othello came back to his wife's room, he was still very angry. He accused her of being unfaithful. He claimed that she was in love with another man, although he would not say any names. Then he began to cry. Desdemona said, "Alas! Why do you weep?"

Othello told her he could have borne all sorts of evils bravely. He could have suffered poverty, and disease, and shame. But Desdemona's infidelity had broken his heart, he said. He called her a weed that looked so fair and smelled so sweet that the sense ached at it. He said that he wished she had never been born. Then he left her room again.

ACT FIVE

The innocent Desdemona was very shocked by Othello's suspicion of her. She was so upset and unhappy that she only desired to sleep. She asked her servant Emilia to make her bed and put her wedding-sheets on it. Then she lay down, expecting Othello to come and join her later.

Desdemona soon fell asleep, and then Othello came back into the bedroom. He was determined to kill the wife whom he believed had been unfaithful to him.

But when he saw her asleep in bed, he decided that he did not want to shed her blood. He did not want to hurt her beautiful white skin. He decided that he would find a gentler way of killing her. "For she must die," Othello said to himself. "If I do not kill her, she will live to deceive more men." Then he kissed the sleeping Desdemona. That kiss was so sweet that he kissed her again. He began to cry, but he said that they were cruel tears.

Othello's kisses woke Desdemona up. Lying in bed, she looked at Othello and saw that his face was grim. He told her to prepare herself for death. He reminded her to say her prayers, because he did not want to kill her soul as well as her body.

The innocent Desdemona begged for her husband's mercy and asked to know why he wanted to kill her. Othello told her that she was the lover of Cassio. He also explained that he knew that she had given Cassio her handkerchief. Confused and desperate, Desdemona told Othello that he was mistaken. She began to plead for her life.

But suddenly, in a fit of anger, Othello refused to hear any more. Grabbing Desdemona, Othello covered her in the bedsheets. He held her down and smothered her to death.

* * * *

At this same moment, Cassio was brought to Othello's house. He was wounded and bleeding because Iago had paid someone to attack him. However, the attack was not successful, and Cassio had survived with only small wounds. In the pockets of the dead attacker, letters that proved the guilt of Iago were found.

This discovery of the letters—and the knowledge of Iago's evil—was like a stroke of thunder to Othello. Suddenly he realized that Iago had made him into a murderer. He realized that his poor, innocent wife had always been faithful to him.

This terrible realization filled Othello with the greatest sadness and regret. Immediately he took out his own sword and killed himself with it. His body fell upon the body of the dead Desdemona.

These tragic events filled all the people of Cyprus and Venice with horror. Othello had always been a very well-respected and honorable man. Until he had been tricked by Iago's evil plot, he had been a kind and loving husband to Desdemona. He had loved not wisely, but too well.

After Othello's death, all his good qualities and heroic actions were remembered. As for Iago, he was immediately put in prison and then killed for his terrible crimes.

King Lear

【キーワード】

☐Dover　　　☐duke　　　☐earl
☐flatter　　　☐loyal　　　☐rude

【あらすじ】

　ブリテンのリア王は年老い、領土を3人の娘に割譲して引退することを決意する。自分を最も愛してくれている娘に一番大きな領土を譲ろうと思い、それぞれに自分への愛の深さを尋ねた。長女と次女は心にもないお世辞をいって領土を得たが、三女コーディリアは率直で正直な返事をして父の機嫌を損ね、相続権を失った。リア王が引退すると、長女と次女は手のひらを返し、老王を冷遇し始めた…。

【主な登場人物】

King Lear　リア王　ブリテンの老王。

Goneril　ゴネリル　リア王の長女。

Regan　リーガン　リア王の次女。

Cordelia　コーディリア　リア王の末娘。父を敬愛している。

Duke of Albany　オールバニー公爵　長女ゴネリルの夫。高潔な人物。

Duke of Cornwall　コーンウォール公爵　次女リーガンの夫。

King or France　フランス王　末娘コーディリアの夫。相続権を失ったコーディリアに態度を変えず求婚した。

Earl of Kent (Caius)　ケント伯爵（ケイアス）　コーディリアを弁護して国外追放されるが、王を守るため姿と名前を変えて国内に留まる。

Edmund　エドマンド　故グロスター伯爵の婚外子。リア王の長女と次女に二股をかけ、王位を狙う。

Edgar　エドガー　故グロスター伯爵の嫡出子。

ACT ONE

King Lear was the King of Britain. He had three daughters. The eldest was named Goneril. The second was named Regan. The youngest daughter, who was her father's favorite, was Cordelia. Goneril was married to the Duke of Albany. Regan was married to the Duke of Cornwall. Cordelia was not yet married, but both the King of France and the Duke of Burgundy wanted to marry her.

King Lear was tired and old. He knew that he would probably die soon, and he did not want to rule the kingdom any longer. He decided to let his daughters rule the kingdom. He planned to give the biggest part of the kingdom to the daughter who loved him the most.

First, King Lear spoke to Goneril, his eldest daughter. He asked, "How much do you love me?"

Goneril replied, "I love you more than words can say. I love you more than the light of my own eyes. I love you more than life. I love you more than liberty!"

But Goneril was lying, and her words were empty. She was just flattering her father.

Old King Lear believed that Goneril was telling the truth, and he was very happy with her answer. He decided to give Goneril and her husband one-third of the kingdom.

Then King Lear turned to his second daughter, Regan. "How much do you love me?" he asked.

Regan answered in the same flattering, lying way as Goneril. She said, "Father, I love you even more than Goneril does. Your love is my only pleasure in life. Nothing else is important to me."

King Lear believed Regan's words. He decided to give Regan and her husband one-third of his kingdom, too.

Then King Lear spoke to his youngest daughter, Cordelia, who was his dearest child. He had always loved her the most. He thought that Cordelia would say that she loved him even more than Goneril and Regan.

But Cordelia was disgusted with the flattery and lies of her sisters. She knew that their words were empty. They were greedy for power and wealth. So Cordelia only said, "I love you according to my duty, neither more nor less."

The king was shocked and upset. He thought that Cordelia was being ungrateful and rude. He warned her to think about what she was saying. "Be careful," King Lear told her. "You will destroy your fortune if you answer me so ungratefully."

But Cordelia answered, "Father, you have given me life and love, and I love you and obey you and honor you greatly. But I cannot speak like my sisters. I cannot make such big speeches. I must speak the truth. If I ever marry, I must give my husband at least half of my love, my care, and my duty. It would not be honest or right to say that you are the only one I love."

In reality, Cordelia loved her father very, very much—much more than Goneril or Regan. But after hearing her greedy sisters' lies and flattery, she thought that the most honorable thing to do was to love and be silent. She did not want to speak words of love in order to get power and wealth.

Old King Lear was very angry. He did not realize that Cordelia's love was true. He decided to punish her. Instead of giving her one-third of the kingdom, he gave her nothing.

The old king divided his kingdom between Goneril and Regan and their husbands, the Dukes of Albany and Cornwall. He announced that they would rule over the kingdom. King Lear would keep his kingly title as a mark of respect. He would also keep one hundred knights to serve him, as a sign of his royal dignity, but he would no longer rule.

* * * *

King Lear's friends were extremely shocked and sad. They felt that Lear had made a very foolish decision by allowing his daughters to rule the kingdom. They also felt that King Lear had acted cruelly and unwisely by disinheriting Cordelia. But they were too scared to do anything or to tell the king their thoughts.

The only person who dared to speak to King Lear was the Earl of Kent. The Earl of Kent loved the king deeply and was very loyal to him. He had always served the king faithfully and given him good advice.

The Earl of Kent told King Lear that Cordelia truly loved him. He told him that Cordelia was a good and respectful daughter. She was too honest to speak flattering words, Kent said, but her love was deep and real.

But King Lear did not want to listen to the Earl of Kent's wise words. Instead he became very angry with Kent, too. He banished the Earl of Kent from his kingdom. King Lear said, "You have five days to leave my kingdom. On the sixth day, if you are still in Britain, I will have you killed."

Even though he knew that the king was making a mistake, the Earl remained an obedient subject. And so the faithful Earl of Kent sadly said goodbye to the king and left the palace.

* * * *

Then King Lear called the King of France and the Duke of Burgundy to him. He asked them if they still wanted to marry Cordelia. "She no longer has any fortune or riches or land," King Lear told the King of France and the Duke of Burgundy. "Cordelia has lost my favor because of her ungrateful words and disrespectful behavior. Do you still wish to marry her?"

The Duke of Burgundy said no. He did not want to marry Cordelia now because she had no land or money.

But the King of France said yes. He still wanted to marry Cordelia. He understood that she truly loved her father but could not speak lies or flattery. He knew that Cordelia was honest and honorable, unlike her two sisters. "Come to France and be my Queen," he said to Cordelia. "I will gladly marry you."

Cordelia agreed to marry the King of France, but she was still sad to leave her father. She was very worried that Goneril and Regan would treat old King Lear badly. "Love our father well, and take good care of him," Cordelia told her sisters. But Goneril and Regan were scornful and did not pay attention.

* * * *

As soon as Cordelia left, Goneril and Regan began to treat their father badly. At first, King Lear was living with Goneril and her husband. But Goneril hated to see King Lear and his one hundred knights. She never wanted to see her father or speak to him. When she did speak to him, she was rude. Soon even Goneril's servants began to treat King Lear rudely.

At first, King Lear tried not to notice Goneril's rudeness. He did not want to admit that he had been wrong about Goneril's love for him. But slowly he began to realize that Goneril did not love him at all.

ACT TWO

Meanwhile, the good and faithful Earl of Kent was still hiding in Britain. Even though the king had banished him, Kent had decided to stay. He wanted to help Lear in any way he could. So Kent disguised himself as a humble servant named Caius. He offered himself to King Lear as a servant. King Lear did not realize that Caius was actually his faithful friend, the Earl of Kent, and so he accepted Caius as a servant.

Caius quickly showed his love of King Lear. He served and protected the old king well. He also defended King Lear against the bad treatment of Goneril and her servants. When Goneril's steward was very rude to King Lear, Caius locked him up. King Lear was very touched by his new servant's loyalty to him. Soon King Lear trusted and loved Caius. He never guessed that Caius was actually his old friend, the Earl of Kent.

King Lear had one more faithful friend, as well. The court jester, or fool, was kind to him. Occasionally the fool made fun of Lear for giving up his kingdom to his daughters. But mostly, the fool told jokes and sang songs to make Lear feel better.

* * * *

Over time, Goneril treated her father more and more badly. She complained that he should not stay with her. She said that it was too costly to take care of him and his one hundred knights. "You must get rid of some of your knights," she told King Lear unkindly. "You have too many. It costs too much to feed and clothe all of them."

King Lear was very surprised to hear Goneril's words. "I gave you my crown and my lands!" he said. "How can be you so ungrateful?"

But Goneril had no love for her father and no respect for his old age. She continued to complain, and King Lear became angry. He decided to leave Goneril's home and go stay with his second daughter Regan.

Goneril's husband, the Duke of Albany, was an honorable man. He felt sorry for the old king. The Duke believed that Goneril was treating her father badly. He asked King Lear to stay. But King Lear was too angry to listen. He and his one hundred knights left to go to Regan's home.

* * * *

As they traveled, King Lear thought fondly of his daughter Cordelia. He realized that he had treated her badly, and he began to cry. He felt shame for his foolish actions, and he regretted giving Goneril so much power over him.

As he traveled, King Lear sent his servant Caius ahead with a letter to Regan, so that she would be ready for his arrival. But unfortunately Goneril had already sent a letter to Regan, too. In her letter, Goneril warned Regan against their father. She claimed that he had been difficult and troublesome. Goneril told Regan that she should not welcome the old king and his one hundred knights.

Caius arrived at the same time as Goneril's evil steward, the same one who had been rude to King Lear. Caius challenged the steward to a fight and beat him. When Regan heard this, she became angry. She punished Caius by putting him in the stocks, even though he was a messenger from her royal father. So the first thing King Lear saw when he arrived at Regan's home was his faithful servant Caius being punished.

ACT THREE

The punishment of Caius made King Lear angry. It was a sign of his daughter Regan's disrespect. She should not have punished a royal messenger from her father.

This lack of respect was followed by more rudeness. Regan and her husband, the Duke of Cornwall, refused to greet King Lear. This disrespect made King Lear even more angry. He insisted on seeing Regan and her husband. When he finally saw them, he discovered that the hated Goneril was also with them.

King Lear asked Regan to let him stay with her. He pleaded with her. But Regan told her father that he could not stay with her. She said that he should go home again with Goneril. "You should do what Goneril says," Regan told the old king. "You should apologize to her. You should give up half of your knights. You are old now, and you need to listen to us. We know better than you," she said disrespectfully.

Regan's cold welcome and unkind words made King Lear very sad. "I will never go back to Goneril's home," Lear said. "I will stay here with my one hundred knights. Do not forget! I gave you half of my kingdom! Where is your respect? Where is your gratitude? Where is your love?"

But Regan had no love for her father. She said, "If you stay with me, you can only have twenty-five knights, not fifty. You do not need so many."

Poor King Lear was shocked by her unkindness. "Then I will go back to Goneril's home," he said. "She will let me have fifty knights, not twenty-five, so she must love me twice as much."

Then cruel Goneril said, "Why do you need even twenty-five knights? Or even ten knights? Or five? Why do you need any at all? It costs too much for me to feed and house them. My servants should be enough for you. You do not need your own." Goneril was determined to take away all of her father's dignity. She had no respect for him, and no gratitude for his generosity to her.

The selfish cruelty of Goneril and Regan was a shock to poor King Lear. At last he realized that these two daughters did not love him at all. Instead, they were greedy and hungry for power. He had been fooled by their lies and flattery. King Lear became so angry that he started to lose his mind and go crazy.

* * * *

Outside, a terrible storm began. Cold rain fell. Thunder and lightning raged. Even though the weather was awful, King Lear did not want to stay with Goneril or Regan. He preferred being outside in the terrible storm, rather than being inside and suffering his daughters' cruelty.

So the old king left Regan's house and went out into the storm. Only the faithful fool and King Lear's servant Caius (who was secretly the Earl of Kent) came with him. After a while, Caius persuaded King Lear to shelter in a small cave, to get away from the storm.

* * * *

In the morning, the Earl of Kent arranged for King Lear to be taken to the castle of Dover, where Kent still had some loyal friends. Those friends would take care of the poor, old, mad king. Lear would be safe in Dover, Kent knew.

Then the Earl of Kent decided to leave Britain. He decided to set sail to France. He went to see the King of France and Cordelia, who was now the king's wife.

ACT FOUR

The Earl of Kent told Cordelia how badly her sisters had treated their father. He explained that poor King Lear had lost his mind because of Goneril and Regan's cruelty. He explained that King Lear was alone and powerless, without his friends or his kingdom.

Cordelia was very upset to hear about her father. Even though King Lear had been very unkind to her, she still loved him. She could not bear to hear that he was alone and suffering. Cordelia decided to go back to Britain to help him.

With the King of France's permission, Cordelia sailed to Britain with the Earl of Kent. She brought the French army with her. Cordelia had a plan: she and her army would fight Goneril and Regan and then restore King Lear to his throne. Soon Cordelia and her army arrived at Dover.

* * * *

After they arrived in Dover, some of Cordelia's soldiers found the old, mad King Lear wandering outside. (He had somehow escaped from the castle of Dover, where Kent's friends had been caring for him.) By now, King Lear had completely lost his mind. He was singing to himself and wearing a crown made of straw and weeds.

Cordelia wanted to see her father right away. However, the doctors told her to wait until they gave King Lear some medicine. The medicine would help his mind. Soon the old king was feeling better, thanks to the doctors. Although he was still half-mad, he was calmer and less confused.

* * * *

When Cordelia finally saw her beloved father, she hugged and kissed him and asked for his blessing. King Lear was just as happy. He cried with joy to see his darling child. With tears in his eyes, he begged for Cordelia's forgiveness.

However, Cordelia told him that there was nothing to forgive. "I love you, and I will kiss you to kiss away all of my sisters' unkindness," Cordelia said. "They should be ashamed of themselves for treating you like that. How could they send their good, kind, old father out into the night and the storm! On such a terrible night, I would not even send my enemy's dog away from my house." Then Cordelia told King Lear that she had come from France to help him.

* * * *

While Cordelia comforted and took care of her poor, half-mad father, her two sisters were still acting in evil ways. Both Goneril and Regan were being unfaithful to their husbands, the Dukes of Albany and of Cornwall. Both sisters had fallen in love with the same man, Edmund. He was the bastard son of the dead Earl of Gloucester.

Edmund was an evil man. He hated his brother Edgar, who was the lawful heir and the next Earl of Gloucester. Edmund had plotted to stop Edgar from inheriting their father's title and wealth.

Edmund's plot against Edgar had worked, and now he was the Earl. Someday he hoped to be king, too. That was why Edmund had seduced both Goneril and Regan. This evil man was also the commander of Goneril and Regan's army that was marching off to fight Cordelia's army.

* * * *

Around this time, the Duke of Cornwall, Regan's husband, died. Immediately Regan announced that she planned to marry Edmund.

When Goneril heard this news, she became very jealous and angry toward her sister. (Edmund had made love to both of the sisters and promised to marry each of them.) Goneril decided to take revenge on Regan. She secretly put poison into her sister's food, killing her.

Unfortunately for Goneril, her evil deed was discovered by her husband, the Duke of Albany. The Duke was a good man. He was very shocked by his wife's actions. As a punishment for murdering her sister, the Duke put Goneril in prison. Full of rage and disappointed love, Goneril soon killed herself. That was the end of these two evil sisters, Regan and Goneril.

ACT FIVE

Tragically, the good and kind Cordelia did not meet a happier end than her cruel sisters. Cordelia's army was fighting the army of Goneril and Regan, which was under the command of Edmund, the bad Earl of Gloucester. Edmund's army won the battle, and Edmund put Cordelia and her father, King Lear, in prison. On Edmund's orders, the innocent Cordelia was murdered in prison.

Heartbroken by his daughter's death, old King Lear died soon afterwards. The loyal Earl of Kent, who served Lear faithfully until his death, also died.

Soon afterwards, the evil Edmund was killed by his good brother Edgar. Edgar then became the true Earl of Gloucester. Since King Lear and all three of his daughters were now dead, the Duke of Albany became the next king of Britain.

Macbeth

【キーワード】

☐ prediction   ☐ spirit   ☐ thane
☐ throne   ☐ tyrant   ☐ witch

【あらすじ】

　スコットランドの武将マクベスとバンクォーは、戦の帰り道に3人の魔女たちから奇妙な予言を伝えられる。曰く、マクベスはやがて王になるという。しかし王位を継ぐのはバンクォーの子孫であるという。マクベスと彼の妻は予言通りに王位を手に入れるべく現王を討つこと、そして手に入れた王位を予言通りに失いはしないかという妄執に取り付かれていく。

【主な登場人物】

Duncan　ダンカン　スコットランドの王。

Macbeth　マクベス　王家の親族。グラームズの領主であり、誉れ高き将軍。

Banquo　バンクォー　マクベスの同僚。スコットランドの将軍。

three women　マクベスとバンクォーが荒野で出会った3名の奇妙な女性たち（魔女）。二人に予言を授ける。

Lady Macbeth　マクベス夫人　美人だが、権力に飢え、夫を王位につかせたくてたまらない腹黒い女性。

Fleance　フリーアンス　バンクォーの息子。

Malcolm　マルコム　ダンカン王の息子。長男。

Donalbain　ドナルベイン　ダンカン王の息子。次男。

Macduff　マクダフ　ファイフの領主。

ACT ONE

When Duncan the Meek was the King of Scotland, there lived a great thane, or lord, called Macbeth. Macbeth was the Thane of Glamis and was related to the king's family. He was admired for his great bravery in war. In fact, he had just helped win an important battle for the king.

Banquo was another Scottish general. He and Macbeth were traveling together, going home from the battle.

* * * *

Late one night, Banquo and Macbeth came to a lonely field. There they saw three people. These people looked like women, but they had beards and wore strange, wild, weird clothing.

Macbeth and Banquo approached them slowly. Then the first strange woman greeted Macbeth by name. She called him the Thane of Glamis. Macbeth was very surprised that she knew his name and title.

Then the second woman spoke. She called Macbeth the Thane of Cawdor. This confused Macbeth, because he was not the Thane of Cawdor. That title did not belong to him.

Finally, the third woman spoke to him: "All hail! Macbeth, you shall be king hereafter!" Macbeth was now extremely shocked and confused. There was no reason that he would ever become king. In fact, King Duncan had two sons who would inherit his throne someday.

Next, the three strange women turned to Banquo and spoke to him. They called to him: "Lesser than Macbeth, and greater! Not so happy, but much happier!" Then they said to Banquo, "You shall never be king. But your children—the children of Banquo—shall be kings of Scotland." Then the three mysterious women disappeared into the air. Banquo and Macbeth quickly realized that these women must have been witches.

Suddenly a messenger from the king arrived. He had a message for Macbeth. He told them that Macbeth had just been named the Thane of Cawdor. Macbeth was amazed: the witches' prediction had come true! He began to wonder if the witches' other prediction would come true, too. Would he, Macbeth, someday become the king of Scotland?

Turning to Banquo, Macbeth asked, "Do you hope that your children will become kings of Scotland someday, as the witches predicted?"

"The witches are creatures of darkness," Banquo answered. "Often they tell us small truths in order to trick us into doing large and terrible things."

But the wicked predictions of the witches were very powerful, and Macbeth did not listen to Banquo's warning. From then on, Macbeth only thought about becoming king of Scotland. He dreamed of having power and glory.

* * * *

Macbeth told his wife about the witches' predictions. His wife was a bad woman. She always wanted more power for herself and Macbeth. She did not care how they got more power.

Lady Macbeth encouraged Macbeth to try to become king. "You must murder the king," she told him. "There is no other way! Then you will become the king." But Macbeth was not as eager as his wife. He was afraid of doing such a terrible murder.

ACT TWO

Not long after, King Duncan visited Macbeth's castle. King Duncan's two sons, his older son Malcolm and his younger son Donalbain, came with him. The visit was to honor Macbeth for his victory in battle.

Macbeth's castle was large and elegant. The king liked it very much and was enjoying his visit there. King Duncan was very pleased by the beauty and politeness of Lady Macbeth, too. She smiled sweetly at the king and treated him with great respect.

But underneath her smiles, Lady Macbeth's heart was black and evil. She was planning to murder the king. Although she looked like an innocent flower, she was in fact like a dangerous snake.

* * * *

That night, King Duncan was tired after his long journey, and so he went to bed early. Two servants guarded him in his bedroom as he slept.

In the middle of the night, everyone was asleep except Lady Macbeth. Outside the world was dark and quiet. Lady Macbeth still wanted to murder the king. However, she was afraid that her husband was too soft and uncertain to murder the king. Macbeth was an ambitious man, but he was still reluctant to do such a terrible deed.

So Lady Macbeth decided to kill the king herself. She went into King Duncan's bedroom with a knife. She saw that the king (and his two servants) were asleep. Lady Macbeth stared at the king. As she stared at him, she thought that he looked a little bit like her father. She lost her courage for a moment and could not kill him.

Unable to do the deed, Lady Macbeth quietly left the king's bedroom. She went to talk to Macbeth and convince him to murder the king.

* * * *

However, Macbeth was becoming reluctant. "There are good reasons not to kill the king," he said to his wife. "First, Duncan is my king, and he is also related to me. Second, I am the king's host—he is staying in my house. It is very wrong for a host to harm his guest.

Third, King Duncan is a good and fair king. He loves his people and treats them well. And if King Duncan is murdered, his people will have to revenge his death. Finally, the murder of a king is a terrible deed. My honor and reputation would forever be destroyed by killing King Duncan."

But Lady Macbeth was determined. "You must kill the king!" she told Macbeth. "You promised that you would do this. You must be brave and keep your promise. Once you promise something, you must do it. If I had made a promise, I would keep it—even if it meant killing the smallest and most innocent child! You must kill the king, and it will be easy to do. Duncan is sleeping and helpless. Also, the murder will be over quickly, in just one night. Then you will be the king for all of our days and nights! Finally, no one will suspect us. We can blame the king's servants."

Lady Macbeth's evil words convinced her husband. So Macbeth got a knife and went quietly into King Duncan's bedroom. Suddenly he saw something strange and frightening in the air: a ghostly knife with blood on it! The handle of the knife was pointing toward him. "Is this a knife I see before me?" Macbeth cried.

But when Macbeth tried to grab the knife, the

strange vision disappeared. "I must have imagined the knife," Macbeth told himself. He tried not to be afraid. He approached the king's bed and quickly killed him with his knife. The king's servants stirred but did not wake up.

Then suddenly Macbeth thought he heard a ghostly voice. The voice seemed to say, "Sleep no more! Macbeth has murdered sleep, the innocent sleep, that feeds life." Then the voice seemed to cry louder. It said, "Sleep no more! Glamis has murdered sleep. Therefore Cawdor shall sleep no more. Macbeth shall sleep no more."

* * * *

Macbeth hurried back to his wife. His mind was full of terrible thoughts. "I have killed the king," he told her.

Lady Macbeth had him wash his hands because they were covered with blood. Meanwhile, she took his knife and put it with the king's servants so it would look like they had killed the king.

* * * *

In the morning, the murder of King Duncan was discovered. Macbeth and Lady Macbeth pretended to be shocked and sad. At first, people thought that the king's servants had killed him. But then, people began to suspect Macbeth. Macbeth had more to gain from the king's death than the two servants did.

Fearing Macbeth, King Duncan's two sons fled. Malcolm, the eldest, went to England. The younger, Donalbain, went to Ireland.

With Malcolm and Donalbain gone, Macbeth was crowned king of Scotland. Thus another prediction of the three witches came true.

ACT THREE

But Macbeth and his new queen could not forget the other prediction of the witches: that although Macbeth should be king, not his children, but the children of Banquo, should be kings after him. This prediction upset them very much. Therefore Macbeth decided to kill both Banquo and his son Fleance. Then the witches' prediction about Banquo's children will not come true, Macbeth thought.

* * * *

So Macbeth and his queen held a special dinner for all the thanes of Scotland, including Banquo and Fleance. As Banquo and Fleance traveled to the dinner, they were attacked by murderers who had been hired by Macbeth. Banquo was killed in the attack, but Fleance escaped.

Later, as the witches had predicted, Fleance's descendants became kings of Scotland, ending with

James the Sixth of Scotland and the First of England.

Meanwhile, at the dinner, Macbeth and his queen acted like gracious royal hosts. Macbeth pretended to wonder where Banquo was. "Where is my good friend Banquo?" Macbeth asked the other lords. "I wonder why he is late."

* * * *

Just then, the ghost of Banquo entered the room. The ghost sat on the chair that belonged to Macbeth. Macbeth's face was white with fear, and he trembled. However, the queen and the other lords could not see the ghost. They thought that Macbeth was staring at an empty chair.

Macbeth began to speak to the ghost. The queen realized that Macbeth was speaking to the murdered Banquo, and she did not want the other lords to hear Macbeth's words. She quickly ended the dinner and sent the other lords away. She told them that Macbeth was feeling ill.

* * * *

But Macbeth and his queen continued to have terrible dreams. Their minds were filled with awful visions and thoughts. The escape of Fleance also upset them, because they knew that Fleance's children would become kings of Scotland someday.

With these miserable thoughts, Macbeth and his queen were never at peace. Their days and night were filled with great worry. And so one night, Macbeth decided to go and see the three strange witches again. He wanted to find out what other predictions they had.

ACT FOUR

Macbeth found the witches in a dark cave in the woods. The witches had known that Macbeth was coming, and so they were ready for him. They did terrible magic to call up spirits to help them predict the future.

In a giant cauldron, the witches mixed together many things. They added toads, bats, snakes, the eye of a newt, the tongue of a dog, the leg of a lizard, the wing of an owl, the scale of a dragon, the tooth of a wolf, and the mouth of a shark.

The witches stirred the cauldron. Then suddenly, three evil spirits appeared. The first spirit told Macbeth, "Beware of Macduff, the Thane of Fife." Macbeth had often been jealous of Macduff, and so he thanked the spirit for the advice.

Then the second spirit spoke to Macbeth. It said, "Do not be afraid, Macbeth. Be bloody and bold, because no one born of a woman will be able to hurt you." Macbeth was very pleased with this. "Then

I have nothing to fear," he said. "But I will still kill Macduff, just to be careful."

Finally, the third spirit spoke to Macbeth. "You shall never be beaten until the Forest of Birnam comes to Dunsinane Hill." These words made Macbeth even happier. "How can a forest move?" he cried. "That is impossible! I am completely safe. I need not worry."

Before he turned to leave, Macbeth cried, "Please, spirits, I must ask you this. Will Banquo's children ever be kings of Scotland?"

Suddenly a ghostly vision appeared to answer his question. Macbeth saw a line of kings, followed by Banquo. In Banquo's hands there was a mirror. The ghostly Banquo smiled and pointed at the mirror, which showed even more kings. Then Macbeth knew that Banquo's children would be kings.

The three witches disappeared, leaving Macbeth angry and filled with bloody thoughts. Despite everything the spirits had said, Banquo's children would still be kings—and Macbeth's children would not.

* * * *

Then Macbeth got terrible news: Macduff, the Thane of Fife, had gone to England. He had joined Malcolm, son of King Duncan. Together Malcolm and Macduff were forming an army to fight Macbeth.

To punish Macduff, Macbeth killed his wife and children and the rest of his family.

This terrible deed made the other Scottish lords angry. Many of them fled to England to join Malcolm and Macduff's army. Everyone hated the evil king Macbeth and began to plot against him.

* * * *

Soon afterwards, Macbeth's wife and queen died. Filled with guilt for her crimes, tortured by terrible dreams, Lady Macbeth killed herself. Then Macbeth was all alone, without even one friend. Soon he began to wish for death for himself.

ACT FIVE

But the army of Malcolm, King Duncan's son, was already marching toward Scotland. They were coming to fight Macbeth. The approaching battle forced Macbeth to summon his courage to fight. He decided that if he had to die, he would die in battle and wearing his armor.

Macbeth's courage was also strengthened by the spirits' predictions. He remembered their words to him: no one born of a woman would be able to hurt him, and he could not be defeated until the Forest of Birnam came to Dunsinane.

Both of those predictions made Macbeth feel confident that he would win the battle. For who had ever heard of a man who was not born of a woman? How could a forest ever move from one place to another? Both things seemed impossible.

And so Macbeth shut himself up in his strongest, safest castle. There he waited for Malcolm's army to arrive.

* * * *

Then one day, a messenger arrived for Macbeth. He was pale and shaking with fear. The messenger said, "I was looking toward Birnam, and suddenly it seemed as if the forest was moving!"

Macbeth was shocked and fearful. "How can this be possible? Is the spirits' prediction coming true?" he wondered. But then he grew determined. "But if I must fight Malcolm, then I will. In truth, I am tired and almost wish that my life were done." So Macbeth called his soldiers and went out to meet Malcolm's army.

* * * *

The strange sight of a forest moving was soon explained. As Malcolm's army marched through the Forest of Birnam, Malcolm ordered his soldiers to cut tree branches and hold them up in front of them. This was a way of hiding the army's size. From a distance, however, the marching soldiers looked like a forest moving. Thus one of the prediction of the spirits came true, and Macbeth began to feel less confident.

* * * *

Then a great battle began between Macbeth's army and Malcolm's army. Malcolm and his army fought well, but the desperate Macbeth fought fiercely, too. He killed many of his enemies.

But then Macbeth saw Macduff. Remembering that the spirits had told him to beware Macduff, Macbeth tried to run away. He wanted to avoid fighting Macduff.

* * * *

But Macduff had been looking for Macbeth throughout the battle. He would not let him run away. "Tyrant! Murderer! You killed my wife and children!" Macduff cried.

Then Macbeth remembered the words of the spirit: how no one born of a woman could hurt him. Smiling confidently, Macbeth answered, "You cannot hurt me, Macduff! I have a charmed life. I cannot be harmed except by the man who is not born of woman."

"Then you should be afraid, for your charmed life is over" Macduff replied. "I was never born of a woman in the ordinary way that men are born. Instead, I was taken from my mother's womb."

Hearing this news, Macbeth began to tremble. He cursed Macduff and cried, "In the future, no man should ever believe the lying words of spirits and witches. They fool us with words that have double meanings... I will not fight you, Macduff!"

"Then live!" said the scornful Macduff. "We will make you into a show, just as men show monsters. We will show you to the people with a sign that says, 'Here men may see the tyrant!'"

"Never!" said Macbeth. His courage returned with his despair. He decided to fight to the death.

"I will not live to kiss the ground at young Malcolm's feet," Macbeth said to Macduff. "Although the forest of Birnam has come to Dunsinane, and even though you are not born of woman, I will still fight you to the death!"

With these last words, Macbeth began to attack Macduff. After a terrible fight, Macduff killed Macbeth and cut off his head.

* * * *

The battle was over. Malcolm's army had won. Macduff gave Macbeth's head as a present to the young king, Malcolm. King Malcolm then took his rightful throne. He ruled over Scotland as his father Duncan had done before him. And thus ended the story of the murderer and tyrant Macbeth.

Word List

- 本文で使われている全ての語を掲載しています(LEVEL 1, 2)。ただし、LEVEL 3 以上は、中学校レベルの語を含みません。
- 語形が規則変化する語の見出しは原形で示しています。不規則変化語は本文中で使われている形になっています。
- 一般的な意味を紹介していますので、一部の語で本文で実際に使われている品詞や意味と合っていないことがあります。
- 品詞は以下のように示しています。

名 名詞	代 代名詞	形 形容詞	副 副詞	動 動詞	助 助動詞
前 前置詞	接 接続詞	間 間投詞	冠 冠詞	略 略語	俗 俗語
頭 接頭語	尾 接尾語	記 記号	関 関係代名詞		

A

- □ **aboard** 前 ~に乗って
- □ **about to** 《be -》まさに~しようとしている、~するところだ
- □ **accept** 動 ①受け入れる ②同意する、認める
- □ **accident** 名 ①(不慮の)事故、災難 ②偶然
- □ **accidentally** 副 偶然に、誤って
- □ **accompany** 動 ①ついていく、つきそう ②(~に)ともなって起こる be accompanied by ~に付き添われる
- □ **accomplish** 動 成し遂げる、果たす
- □ **according** 副《- to ~》~によれば[よると]
- □ **according to** ~に従って
- □ **accuse** 動《- of ~》~(の理由)で告訴[非難]する accuse oneself 自分を責める
- □ **ache** 動 ①痛む、うずく ②心を痛める、つらい思いをする
- □ **achieve** 動 成し遂げる、達成する、成功を収める
- □ **act** 名 ①行為、行い ②(演劇・歌劇などの)幕、段 動 ①行動する ②機能する ③演じる act as if ~であるかのように振る舞う
- □ **activity** 名 活動、活気
- □ **actor** 名 俳優、役者
- □ **actually** 副 実際に、本当に、実は
- □ **add** 動 ①加える、足す ②足し算をする ③言い添える
- □ **addition** 名 ①付加、追加、添加 ②足し算 in addition 加えて、さらに
- □ **admire** 動 感心する、賞賛する
- □ **admit** 動 認める、許可する、入れる
- □ **adventure** 名 冒険
- □ **advice** 名 忠告、助言、意見
- □ **advisor** 名 忠告者、助言者、顧問
- □ **afraid of** 《be -》~を恐れる、~を怖がる
- □ **after a while** しばらくして
- □ **afterwards** 副 その後、のちに
- □ **agree with** (人)に同意する
- □ **alarm-bell** 名 警鐘
- □ **alas** 間 ああ《悲嘆・後悔・恐れなどを表す声》
- □ **Albany, Duke of** オールバニー公爵
- □ **All hail!** 万歳！

WORD LIST

- **allow** 動 ①許す,《 – … to ~》…が~するのを可能にする,…に~させておく ②与える
- **alone** 形 leave ~ alone ~をそっとしておく
- **although** 接 ~だけれども, ~にもかかわらず, たとえ~でも
- **amazed** 形 びっくりした, 驚いた
- **ambitious** 形 ①大望のある, 野心的な ②熱望して
- **angel** 名 ①天使 ②天使のような人
- **anger** 名 怒り 動 怒る, ~を怒らせる
- **angrily** 副 怒って, 腹立たしげに
- **announce** 動 (人に)知らせる, 公表する
- **anymore** 副 《通例否定文, 疑問文で》今はもう, これ以上, これから
- **anyone** 代 ①《疑問文・条件節で》誰か ②《否定文で》誰も(~ない) ③《肯定文で》誰でも
- **apart** 副 ①ばらばらに, 離れて ②別にして, それだけで pull ~ apart ~を引き離す
- **Apollo** 名 アポロ《ギリシャ神話》
- **apologize** 動 謝る, わびる
- **apology** 名 謝罪, 釈明
- **appear** 動 ①現れる, 見えてくる ②(~のように)見える, ~らしい appear to ~するように見える
- **approach** 動 ①接近する ②話を持ちかける
- **approve** 動 賛成する, 承認する approve of ~を承認する
- **armor** 名 よろい, かぶと, 甲冑
- **army** 名 軍隊,《the – 》陸軍
- **arrange** 動 ①並べる, 整える ②取り決める ③準備する, 手はずを整える arrange for ~の手配をする
- **arrival** 名 ①到着 ②到達
- **as** 熟 as for ~に関しては, ~はどうかと言うと as if あたかも~のように, まるで~みたいに as much as ~と同じだけ as soon as ~するとすぐ, ~するや否や as well なお, その上, 同様にも just as (ちょうど)であろうとおり not so ~ as … …ほど~でない see ~ as … ~を…と考える
- **ashamed** 形 恥じた, 気が引けた,《be – of ~》~が恥ずかしい, ~を恥じている
- **ask ~ if** ~かどうか尋ねる
- **asleep** 形 眠って(いる状態の) fall asleep 眠り込む, 寝入る
- **attack** 動 ①襲う, 攻める ②非難する 名 攻撃, 非難
- **attacker** 名 ①攻撃者, 敵 ②(球技の)アタッカー
- **attention** 名 ①注意, 集中 ②配慮, 手当て, 世話 pay attention to ~に注意を払う
- **avoid** 動 避ける, (~を)しないようにする
- **awaken** 動 ①目を覚まさせる, 起こす, 目覚める ②《 – to ~》~に気づく
- **awful** 形 ①ひどい, 不愉快な ②恐ろしい

B

- **back** 熟 bring back 戻す, 呼び戻す, 持ち帰る come back 戻る come back to ~へ帰ってくる, ~に戻る
- **badly** 副 ①悪く, まずく, へたに ②とても, ひどく treat someone badly (人)にひどい仕打ちをする
- **banish** 動 追放する, 追い払う
- **Banquo** 名 バンクォー《人名》
- **Baptista** 名 バプティスタ《人名》
- **bastard** 形 非嫡子の
- **bat** 名 コウモリ
- **battle** 名 戦闘, 戦い 動 戦う

- **bear** 動 耐える
- **beard** 名 あごひげ
- **beat** 動 ①打つ, 鼓動する ②打ち負かす
- **beaten** 動 beat (打つ) の過去分詞
- **beauty** 名 ①美, 美しい人[物] ②《the -》美点
- **because of** ～のために, ～の理由で
- **beckon** 動 ①招く, 手招きする ②合図する beckon to (人)に手招きする
- **bed** 熟 go to bed 床につく, 寝る
- **bedroom** 名 寝室
- **bedsheet** 名 敷布
- **beg** 動 懇願する, お願いする beg for mercy 慈悲を請う
- **begin with** ～で始まる
- **behalf** 名 利益 on one's behalf ～のために
- **behave** 動 振る舞う
- **behavior** 名 振る舞い, 態度, 行動
- **behind** 前 ①～の後ろに, ～の背後に ②～に遅れて, ～に劣って reason behind ～の背後にある理由
- **believe in** ～を信じる
- **bell** 名 ベル, 鈴, 鐘
- **belong** 動《- to ～》～に属する, ～のものである
- **beloved** 形 最愛の
- **below** 下に[へ]
- **betray** 動 裏切る, 背く, だます
- **better** 熟 feel better 気分がよくなる
- **beware** 動 用心する, 注意する beware of ～に気を付ける
- **Birnam, Forest of** バーナムの森
- **bit** 名 ①小片, 少量 ②《a -》少し, ちょっと
- **bite** 動 かむ, かじる 名 かむこと, かみ傷, ひと口
- **bitten** 動 bite (かむ) の過去分詞
- **bitterness** 名 ①苦さ ②うらみ, 敵意
- **black-skinned** 形 肌の色が黒い
- **blame** 動 とがめる, 非難する
- **bleed** 動 出血する, 血を流す[流させる]
- **blessing** 名 ①(神の)恵み, 加護 ②祝福の祈り ③(食前・食後の)祈り
- **blood** 名 ①血, 血液 ②血統, 家柄 ③気質 shed someone's blood (人)の血を流す
- **bloody** 形 血だらけの, 血なまぐさい, むごい bloody deed 血なまぐさい事件
- **bold** 形 ①勇敢な, 大胆な, 奔放な ②ずうずうしい
- **borne** 動 bear (負う, 耐える) の過去分詞
- **both of them** 彼ら[それら]両方とも
- **Brabantio** 名 ブラバンショー
- **brain** 名 ①脳 ②知力
- **branch** 名 枝
- **brave** 形 勇敢な
- **bravely** 副 勇敢に(も)
- **bravery** 名 勇敢さ, 勇気ある行動
- **brawl** 名 乱闘
- **breath** 名 息, 呼吸
- **bridal** 形 花嫁の, 婚礼の
- **bring back** 戻す, 呼び戻す, 持ち帰る
- **Britain** 名 大ブリテン(島)
- **brook** 名 小川
- **Burgundy, Duke of** バーガンディー公爵
- **bury** 動 ①埋葬する, 埋める ②覆い隠す

WORD LIST

C

- □ **Caius** 名 ケイアス《人名》
- □ **call on** 呼びかける, 招集する, 求める, 訪問する
- □ **call to** ～に声をかける
- □ **call up** 呼び出す
- □ **calm** 形 穏やかな, 落ち着いた
- □ **calmly** 副 落ち着いて, 静かに
- □ **care** 熟 care for ～の世話をする, ～を扱う, ～が好きである, ～を大事に思う take care of ～の世話をする, ～面倒を見る, ～を管理する take good care of ～を大事に扱う, 大切にする
- □ **case** 熟 in any case とにかく in case ～だといけないので, 念のため, 万が一
- □ **Cassio, Michael** マイケル・キャシオ《人名》
- □ **castle of Dover** ドーヴァー城
- □ **cauldron** 名 大釜
- □ **cave** 名 洞穴, 洞窟
- □ **Cawdor** 名 コーダ《地名》
- □ **celebrate** 動 ①祝う, 祝福する ②祝典を開く
- □ **celebration** 名 ①祝賀 ②祝典, 儀式
- □ **certain** 形 ①確実な, 必ず～する ②(人が)確信した
- □ **challenge** 動 挑む, 試す
- □ **charge** 動 ①(代金を)請求する ②(～を…に)負わせる ③命じる charge forward 進撃する, 突進する
- □ **charmed** 形 魔法をかけられた charmed life 不死身
- □ **cheer for** ～に声援を送る
- □ **cheerfully** 副 陽気に, 快活に
- □ **chief** 形 最高位の, 第一の, 主要な chief counselor 宰相
- □ **choice** 名 選択(の範囲・自由), 選ばれた人[物]
- □ **claim** 動 ①主張する ②要求する, 請求する
- □ **Claudius** 名 クローディアス《人名》
- □ **clever** 形 ①頭のよい, 利口な ②器用な, 上手な
- □ **cleverly** 副 如才なく, 巧妙に
- □ **closed** 形 閉じた, 閉鎖した
- □ **clothe** 動 服を着せる, 《受け身形で》(～を)着ている, (～の)格好をする
- □ **clothing** 名 衣類, 衣料品
- □ **come** 熟 come and ～しに行く come back 戻る come back to ～へ帰ってくる, ～に戻る come to an end 終わる come true 実現する come upon (偶然)～に出会う
- □ **comfort** 動 心地よくする, ほっとさせる, 慰める
- □ **command** 動 命令する, 指揮する 名 命令, 指揮(権)
- □ **commander** 名 司令官, 指揮官
- □ **commit** 動 ①委託する ②引き受ける ③(罪などを)犯す commit a crime 罪を犯す
- □ **compare** 動 ①比較する, 対照する ②たとえる
- □ **complain** 動 ①不平[苦情]を言う, ぶつぶつ言う ②(病状などを)訴える
- □ **completely** 副 完全に, すっかり
- □ **condemn** 動 ①責める ②有罪と判決する condemn someone to death (人)に死刑を宣告する
- □ **confess** 動 (隠し事などを)告白する, 打ち明ける, 白状する
- □ **confident** 形 自信のある, 自信に満ちた
- □ **confidently** 副 確信して, 自信をもって, 大胆に
- □ **confused** 形 困惑した, 混乱した
- □ **consider** 動 ①考慮する, ～しようと思う ②(～と)みなす ③気にかけ

る, 思いやる
- **contain** 動 ①含む, 入っている ②(感情などを)抑える
- **control** 動 ①管理[支配]する ②抑制する, コントロールする
- **conversation** 名 会話, 会談
- **convince** 動 納得させる, 確信させる be convinced by ～に納得する
- **Cordelia** 名 コーディリア《人名》
- **Cornwall, Duke of** コーンウォール公爵
- **cost** 動 (金・費用が)かかる, (～を)要する, (人に金額を)費やさせる
- **costly** 形 高価な, ぜいたくな, 高くつく
- **could** 熟 Could you ～？ ～してくださいますか。How could ～？何だって～なんてことがありえようか？ If +《主語》+ could ～できればなあ《仮定法》 could have done ～だったかもしれない《仮定法》
- **counselor** 名 カウンセラー, 相談役, 参事官, 弁護士 chief counselor 宰相
- **courage** 名 勇気, 度胸 summon courage to 勇気を奮い起こして～する
- **court** 名 宮廷, 宮殿
- **court jester** 宮廷道化師
- **courtship** 名 求婚期間
- **cover** 動 ①覆う, 包む, 隠す ②扱う, (～に)わたる, 及ぶ ③代わりを務める ④補う be covered with ～でおおわれている
- **crazy** 形 ①狂気の, ばかげた, 無茶な ②夢中の, 熱狂的な
- **creature** 名 (神の)創造物, 生物, 動物
- **crime** 名 ①(法律上の)罪, 犯罪 ②悪事, よくない行為 commit a crime 罪を犯す
- **criticize** 動 ①非難する, あら探しをする ②酷評する ③批評する
- **crown** 動 戴冠する[させる]
- **cruel** 形 残酷な, 厳しい
- **cruelly** 副 残酷に
- **cruelty** 名 残酷さ, 残酷な行為[言動・言葉]
- **cry out** 叫ぶ
- **cure** 動 治療する, 矯正する, 取り除く
- **curl** 名 巻き毛
- **curse** 動 のろう, ののしる
- **cut off** 切断する, 切り離す
- **Cyprus** 名 サイプラス島

D

- **dare** 動《－to ～》思い切って[あえて]～する 助 思い切って[あえて]～する
- **darkness** 名 暗さ, 暗やみ
- **darling** 名 ①最愛の人 ②あなた《呼びかけ》
- **deadly** 形 命にかかわる, 痛烈な, 破壊的な
- **death** 名 ①死, 死ぬこと ②《the －》終え, 消滅 condemn someone to death (人)に死刑を宣告する fight to the death 死ぬまで戦う put to death 処刑する to death 死ぬまで, 死ぬほど
- **deceive** 動 だます, あざむく
- **decision** 名 ①決定, 決心 ②判決
- **decorate** 動 飾る
- **deed** 名 行為, 行動 bloody deed 血なまぐさい事件 evil deed 悪行
- **deeply** 副 深く, 非常に
- **defeat** 動 ①打ち破る, 負かす ②だめにする be defeated by ～に敗れる
- **defend** 動 防ぐ, 守る, 弁護する
- **demand** 動 ①要求する, 尋ねる ②必要とする 名 ①要求, 請求 ②需

WORD LIST

要 demand for ～の要求
- **Denmark** 名 デンマーク《国名》
- **depressed** 形 がっかりした, 落胆した
- **depression** 名 憂うつ, 意気消沈
- **descendant** 名 子孫, 末えい
- **describe** 動 (言葉で)描写する, 特色を述べる, 説明する
- **Desdemona** 名 デズデモーナ《人名》
- **deserve** 動 (～を)受けるに足る, 値する, (～して)当然である
- **desire** 動 強く望む, 欲する
- **despair** 名 絶望, 自暴自棄
- **desperate** 形 ①絶望的な, 見込みのない ②ほしくてたまらない, 必死の
- **despite** 前 ～にもかかわらず
- **destroy** 動 破壊する, 絶滅させる, 無効にする
- **determine** 動 ①決心する[させる] ②決定する[させる] ③測定する
- **determined** 形 決心した, 決然とした
- **differently** 副 (～と)異なって, 違って
- **dignity** 名 威厳, 品位, 尊さ, 敬意
- **dirt** 名 ①汚れ, 泥, ごみ ②土 ③悪口, 中傷
- **disappear** 動 見えなくなる, 姿を消す, なくなる
- **disappointed** 形 がっかりした, 失望した
- **discovery** 名 発見
- **disease** 名 ①病気 ②(社会や精神の)不健全な状態
- **disgraceful** 形 恥ずべき, 不名誉な
- **disguise** 動 変装させる, 隠す 名 変装(すること), 見せかけ in disguise 変装した
- **disgusted** 形 むかついた, 吐き気を催させる be disgusted with ～にうんざりする
- **dishonest** 形 不誠実な
- **disinherit** 動 相続権を奪う
- **displease** 動 不快にする
- **disrespect** 名 尊敬を欠くこと
- **disrespectful** 形 無礼な
- **disrespectfully** 副 無礼に
- **distance** 名 距離, 隔たり, 遠方
- **distract** 動 (注意などを)そらす, まぎらす
- **divide** 動 分かれる, 分ける, 割れる, 割る
- **Donalbain** 名 ドナルベイン《人名》
- **done** 熟 well done うまくやった
- **double** 形 ①2倍の, 二重の ②対の double meaning 二重の意味
- **doubt** 名 ①疑い, 不確かなこと ②未解決点, 困難 動 疑う
- **Dover** 名 ドーヴァー《地名》
- **Dover, castle of** ドーヴァー城
- **drag** 動 ①引きずる ②のろのろ動く[動かす]
- **dragon** 名 竜, ドラゴン
- **draw** 動 ①引く, 引っ張る ②描く ③引き分けになる[する] drawing near ～が近づいている
- **dream of** ～を夢見る
- **drinking** 名 飲むこと, 飲酒
- **duel** 名 決闘
- **duke** 名 公爵
- **Duke of Albany** オールバニー公爵
- **Duke of Burgundy** バーガンディー公爵
- **Duke of Cornwall** コーンウォール公爵
- **Duncan the Meek** 柔和王ダンカン

- **Dunsinane Hill** ダンシネーンの丘
- **duty** 名 ①義務(感),責任 ②職務,任務,関税
- **dying** 形死にかかっている,消えそうな lie dying 死にかけている

E

- **eager** 形 ①熱心な ②《be-for ～》～を切望している,《be-to ～》しきりに～したがっている
- **earl** 名伯爵
- **Earl of Gloucester** グロスター伯爵
- **Earl of Kent** ケント伯爵
- **earnestly** 副まじめに
- **easily** 副 ①容易に,たやすく,苦もなく ②気楽に
- **Edgar** 名エドガー《人名》
- **edge** 名 ①刃 ②端,縁 on the edge of まさに～しようとして
- **Edmund** 名エドマンド《人名》
- **education** 名教育,教養
- **Egyptian** 形エジプト(人,語)の 名 ①エジプト人 ②エジプト語
- **eldest** 形最年長の
- **elegant** 形上品な,優雅な
- **Emilia** 名エミリア《人名》
- **encourage** 動 ①勇気づける ②促進する,助長する
- **end** 熟 come to an end 終わる end with ～で終了する
- **enemy** 名敵
- **England** 名 ①イングランド ②英国
- **enjoyment** 名楽しむこと,喜び
- **entirely** 副完全に,まったく
- **erase** 動 ①消える ②消去する,抹消する
- **escape** 動逃げる,免れる,もれる 名逃亡,脱出,もれ
- **even if** たとえ～でも
- **even though** ～であるけれども,～にもかかわらず
- **every** 熟 in every way すべての点で
- **everyone** 代誰でも,皆
- **everything** 代すべてのこと[もの],何でも,何もかも
- **evil** 形 ①邪悪な ②有害な,不吉な evil deed 悪行 名 ①邪悪 ②害,わざわい,不幸
- **excellent** 形優れた,優秀な
- **excellently** 副見事に
- **except** 前 ～を除いて,～のほかは 接 ～ということを除いて
- **exciting** 形興奮させる,わくわくさせる
- **exclaim** 動 ①(喜び・驚きなどで)声をあげる ②声高に激しく言う
- **expect** 動予期[予測]する,(当然のこととして)期待する
- **extremely** 副非常に,極度に

F

- **fact** 熟 in fact つまり,実は,要するに
- **fair** 形 ①正しい,公平[正当]な ②快晴の ③色白の,金髪の ④かなりの ⑤《古》美しい
- **faithful** 形忠実な,正確な
- **faithfully** 副忠実に,正確に
- **fall asleep** 眠り込む,寝入る
- **fall down** 落ちる,転ぶ
- **fall in love with** 恋におちる
- **fall into** ～に陥る,～してしまう
- **fall upon** ～の上にかかる
- **fallen** 動 fall(落ちる)の過去分詞

Word List

- **false** 形 うその, 間違った, にせの, 不誠実な
- **far** 熟 go too far 行き過ぎる, 度が過ぎる
- **fascinate** 動 魅惑する, うっとりさせる
- **fear** 名 ①恐れ ②心配, 不安 in fear おどおどして, ビクビクして with fear 怖がって 動 ①恐れる ②心配する
- **fearful** 形 ①恐ろしい ②心配な, 気づかって
- **feast** 名 饗宴
- **feed** 動 ①食物を与える ②供給する
- **feel better** 気分がよくなる
- **feel guilty** 気がとがめる
- **feel sick** 気分が悪い
- **feel sorry for** ～をかわいそうに思う
- **fiercely** 副 どう猛に, 猛烈に
- **Fife** 名 ファイフ《地名》
- **fight to the death** 死ぬまで戦う
- **figure** 名 人[物]の姿, 形
- **filled with** 《be－》～でいっぱいになる
- **final** 形 最後の, 決定的な
- **find out** 見つけ出す, 気がつく, 知る, 調べる, 解明する
- **find ～ in** ～を…で見つける
- **fit** 名 発作, けいれん, 一時的興奮
- **flatter** 動 (人)にこびへつらう
- **flattering** 形 へつらいの, お世辞の
- **flattery** 名 へつらい, お世辞, おべっか
- **Fleance** 名 フリーアンス《人名》
- **fled** 動 flee (逃げる) の過去, 過去分詞
- **float** 動 ①浮く, 浮かぶ ②漂流する
- **followed by** その後に～が続いて
- **fond** 形 ①《be－ of ～》～が大好きである ②愛情の深い
- **fondly** かわいがって think fondly of (人)のことを愛情を込めて考える
- **fool** 名 ①ばか者, おろかな人 ②道化師 動 ばかにする, だます, ふざける be fooled by ～にだまされる
- **foolish** 形 おろかな, ばかばかしい
- **force** 動 ①強制する, 力ずくで～する, 余儀なく～させる ②押しやる, 押し込む be forced to ～せざるを得ない
- **forehead** 名 ひたい
- **Forest of Birnam** バーナムの森
- **forgetful** 形 忘れっぽい, 無頓着な
- **forgive** 許す, 免除する
- **forgiveness** 名 許す(こと), 寛容
- **form** 動 形づくる
- **fortune** 名 ①富, 財産 ②幸運, 繁栄, チャンス ③運命, 運勢
- **forward** 副 ①前方に ②将来に向けて ③先へ, 進んで charge forward 突進する
- **France** 名 フランス《国名》
- **freely** 副 自由に, 障害なしに
- **French** 形 フランス(人・語)の 名 ①フランス語 ②《the－》フランス人
- **friendly** 形 親しみのある, 親切な, 友情のこもった
- **friendship** 名 友人であること, 友情
- **frightened** 形 おびえた, びっくりした be frightened by ～におびえる
- **frightening** 形 恐ろしい, どきっとさせる
- **from that time on** あれから, あの時以来

- **from then on** それ以来
- **front** 熟 in front of ~の前に, ~の正面に
- **full of** 《be –》~で一杯である
- **fun** 熟 make fun of ~を物笑いの種にする, からかう
- **funeral** 名 葬式, 葬列
- **furious** 形 怒り狂った, 激怒した, 激しい
- **future** 熟 in the future 将来は

G

- **gain** 動 ①得る, 増す ②進歩する, 進む gain from ~で利益を得る
- **general** 名 大将, 将軍
- **generosity** 名 ①寛大, 気前のよさ ②豊富さ
- **gentle** 形 ①優しい, 温和な ②柔らかな
- **gently** 副 親切に, 上品に, そっと, 優しく
- **Gertrude** 名 ガートルード《人名》
- **get away** 逃げる, 逃亡する, 離れる
- **get rid of** ~を取り除く, 解雇する
- **get someone to do** (人)に~させる[してもらう]
- **get upset** 取り乱す
- **ghost** 名 幽霊
- **ghostly** 形 幽霊のような, ぼんやりした
- **giant** 形 巨大な, 偉大な
- **gift** 名 贈り物
- **give away** ただで与える, 贈る
- **give up** あきらめる, やめる, 引き渡す
- **glad to do** 《be –》~してうれしい, 喜んで~する
- **gladly** 副 喜んで, うれしそうに
- **Glamis** 名 グラームズ《地名》
- **glory** 名 栄光, 名誉, 繁栄
- **Gloucester, Earl of** グロスター伯爵
- **go mad** 発狂する
- **go out** 外出する, 外へ出る
- **go to bed** 床につく, 寝る
- **go too far** 行き過ぎる, 度が過ぎる
- **Goneril** 名 ゴネリル《人名》
- **Gonzago** 名 ゴンザゴー《人名》
- **good** 熟 take good care of ~を大事に扱う, 大切にする
- **goodness** 名 善良さ, よいところ
- **gotten** 動 get(得る)の過去分詞
- **grab** 動 ①ふいにつかむ, ひったくる ②横取りする grab ~ by the throat ~の喉元をつかむ
- **gracious** 形 ①親切な, ていねいな ②慈悲深い ③優雅な
- **gratitude** 名 感謝(の気持ち), 報恩の念
- **grave** 名 墓 open grave 墓穴
- **greatly** 副 大いに
- **greatness** 名 ①偉大さ ②大きいこと, 重要
- **greedy** 形 どん欲である, 欲深い
- **greet** 動 ①あいさつする ②(喜んで)迎える greet someone by name (人)の名前を呼びながら挨拶する
- **grief** 名 (深い)悲しみ, 悲嘆
- **grim** 形 ①(表情などが)険しい, こわい ②厳しい, 残酷な
- **ground** 熟 kiss the ground 地面にキスする
- **grow weak** 弱る
- **guard** 名 ①警戒, 見張り ②番人 動 番をする, 監視する, 守る
- **guest** 名 客, ゲスト
- **guilt** 名 罪, 有罪, 犯罪

WORD LIST

- **guilty** 形 有罪の, やましい feel guilty 気がとがめる

H

- **hail** 動 ①歓呼して迎える, 歓迎する ②合図をおくる **All hail!** 万歳！
- **half-mad** 形 半分狂っている, 半狂乱の
- **Hamlet** 名 ハムレット《人名》
- **handkerchief** 名 ハンカチ
- **handle** 名 取っ手, 握り
- **handsome** 形 端正な(顔立ちの), りっぱな, (男性が)ハンサムな
- **hang** 動 かかる, かける, つるす, ぶら下がる
- **happiness** 名 幸せ, 喜び
- **harm** 動 傷つける, 損なう
- **hate** 動 嫌う, 憎む, (〜するのを)いやがる
- **have** 熟 could have done 〜だったかもしれない《仮定法》 have a headache 頭痛がする have someone do (人)に〜させる[してもらう] should have done 〜すべきだった(のにしなかった)《仮定法》 will have done 〜してしまっているだろう《未来完了形》
- **headache** 名 頭痛 have a headache 頭痛がする
- **hear about** 〜について聞く
- **hear of** 〜について聞く
- **heart** 熟 win someone's heart (人)のハートを射止める
- **heartbroken** 形 悲しみに打ちひしがれた
- **heaven** 名 ①天国 ②《H-》神
- **Hecuba** 名 ヘキュバ《人名》
- **heir** 名 相続人, 後継者
- **helpful** 形 役に立つ, 参考になる
- **helpless** 形 無力の, 自分ではどうすることもできない
- **hereafter** 副 今後は, 将来は
- **heroic** 形 ヒーローの, 英雄の, 勇敢な
- **hide** 動 隠れる, 隠す, 隠れて見えない, 秘密にする
- **hire** 動 雇う, 賃借りする
- **hold up** ①維持する, 支える ②〜を持ち上げる
- **honest** 形 ①正直な, 誠実な, 心からの ②公正な, 感心な
- **honestly** 副 正直に
- **honor** 名 ①名誉, 光栄, 信用 ②節操, 自尊心 a sense of honor 廉恥心 動 尊敬する, 栄誉を与える
- **honorable** 形 ①尊敬すべき, 立派な ②名誉ある ③高貴な
- **honorably** 副 見事に, 立派に
- **Horatio** 名 ホレイシオ《人名》
- **horror** 名 ①恐怖, ぞっとすること ②嫌悪
- **host** 名 客をもてなす主人
- **How could 〜?** 何だって〜なんてことがありえようか？
- **however** 接 けれども, だが
- **hug** 動 しっかりと抱き締める
- **human nature** 人間性
- **humble** 形 つつましい, 粗末な
- **hung over** 〜の上に張り出す
- **hungry for** 《be-》〜に飢えた
- **hurry out of** 大急ぎで〜から出る

I

- **I wish 〜 were …** 私が〜なら…なのに。《仮定法過去》
- **Iago** 名 イアーゴー《人名》
- **if** 熟 act as if 〜であるかのように振る舞う as if あたかも〜のように, まるで〜みたいに ask 〜 if 〜かどう

か尋ねる even if たとえ〜でも If + 《主語》+ could 〜できればなあ《仮定法》if someone ever もし〜なら not know if 〜かどうかわからない see if 〜かどうかを確かめる what if もし〜だったらどうなるだろう wonder if 〜ではないかと思う

- **ignore** 動 無視する、怠る
- **imagine** 動 想像する、心に思い描く
- **immediately** 副 すぐに、〜するやいなや
- **impatiently** 副 我慢できずに、いらいらして wait impatiently イライラして待つ
- **improper** 形 不適切な、妥当でない
- **including** 前 〜を含めて、込みで
- **infidelity** 名 不貞
- **inherit** 動 相続する、受け継ぐ
- **innocent** 形 無邪気な、無実の
- **insist** 動 ①主張する、断言する ②要求する insist on 〜を強く主張[要求]する
- **instantly** 副 すぐに、即座に
- **instead** 副 その代わりに instead of 〜の代わりに、〜をしないで
- **intelligent** 形 頭のよい、聡明な
- **interested** 形 興味を持った、関心のある be interested in 〜に興味[関心]がある
- **Ireland** 名 アイルランド《国名》
- **irresponsible** 形 責任感のない
- **It is 〜 for someone to …** (人)が…するのは〜だ
- **Italian** 形 イタリア(人・語)の 名 ①イタリア人 ②イタリア語

J

- **James the Sixth of Scotland and the First of England** スコットランド王ジェームズ6世およびイングランド王ジェームズ1世
- **jealous** 形 嫉妬して、嫉妬深い、うらやんで be jealous of 〜をねたんでいる
- **jealousy** 名 嫉妬、ねたみ
- **jester** 名 (中世の王侯や貴族に仕えた)道化師 court jester 宮廷道化師
- **joke** 名 冗談、ジョーク
- **journey** 名 ①(遠い目的地への)旅 ②行程
- **joy** 名 喜び、楽しみ
- **judge** 動 判決を下す、裁く、判断する、評価する
- **judgment** 名 ①判断、意見 ②裁判、判決
- **jump into** 〜に飛び込む
- **jump up** 素早く立ち上がる
- **Jupiter** 名 ジュピター《ローマ神話》
- **just as** (ちょうど)であろうとおり
- **just then** そのとたんに

K

- **keep one's promise** 約束を守る
- **keep someone from** 〜から(人)を阻む
- **keep 〜 secret** 〜を秘密にする
- **Kent, Earl of** ケント伯爵
- **kind of** 〜のようなもの[人]
- **kindly** 副 親切に、優しく
- **kindness** 名 親切(な行為)、優しさ
- **King Lear** リア王
- **King of France** フランス王
- **kingdom** 名 王国
- **kingly** 形 王にふさわしい、王の、王

Word List

族の
- **kiss** 名キス 動キスする **kiss away** キスで取り去る **kiss the ground** 地面にキスする
- **knife** 名ナイフ, 小刀, 包丁, 短剣
- **knight** 名騎士, ナイト爵位の人
- **know** 熟 **know of** ～について知っている **not know if** ～かどうかわからない
- **knowledge** 名知識, 理解, 学問

L

- **lack** 名不足, 欠乏
- **Laertes** 名レアーティーズ《人名》
- **last** 熟 **at last** ついに, とうとう
- **lawful** 形合法な
- **lay** 動 lie (横たわる) の過去
- **lead to** ～に至る, ～に通じる, ～を引き起こす
- **Lear, King** リア王
- **least** 名最小, 最少 **at least** 少なくとも
- **leave** 熟 **leave ～ alone** ～をそっとしておく **turn to leave** その場を去ろうと振り返る
- **less** 形～より小さい[少ない] 副～より少なく, ～ほどでなく **neither more nor less** 超えることも下回ることもない
- **liar** 名うそつき
- **liberty** 名自由, 解放
- **lie** 動 ①うそをつく ②横たわる, 寝る ③(ある状態に)ある, 存在する **lie down** 横たわる, 横になる **lie dying** 死にかけている 名うそ, 詐欺
- **lieutenant** 名 ①中尉, 少尉 ②代理, 副官
- **life** 熟 **charmed life** 不死身
- **lift** 動持ち上げる, 上がる
- **lightning** 名電光, 雷, 稲妻
- **light-skinned** 形肌が白い
- **like** 熟 **look like** ～のように見える, ～に似ている
- **line of** ～の系統, 血筋, 一連の
- **lived** 熟 **there lived ～.** ～が住んでいた
- **lizard** 名トカゲ
- **lock someone up** ～を監禁する
- **lonely** 形 ①孤独な, 心さびしい ②ひっそりした, 人里離れた
- **longer** 熟 **no longer** もはや～でない[～しない]
- **look for** ～を探す
- **look like** ～のように見える, ～に似ている
- **lord** 名首長, 主人, 領主, 貴族, 上院議員 **my lord** 夫, 主人
- **lose one's mind** 気が狂う
- **love** 熟 **be in love with** ～に恋して, ～に心を奪われて **fall in love with** 恋におちる **make love** 恋の営みをする
- **lover** 名 ①愛人, 恋人 ②愛好者
- **loving** 形愛する, 愛情のこもった
- **loyal** 形忠実な, 誠実な
- **loyalty** 名忠義, 忠誠
- **Lucianus** 名ルシアーナス《人名》
- **lying** 動 lie (うそをつく・横たわる) の現在分詞 形 ①うそをつく, 虚偽の ②横になっている

M

- **Macbeth** 名マクベス《人名》
- **Macduff** 名マクダフ《人名》
- **mad** 形 ①気の狂った ②逆上した, 理性をなくした ③ばかげた ④(～に)熱狂[熱中]して, 夢中の **go mad** 発狂する
- **madman** 名 ①狂人 ②常軌を逸

した人

- **madness** 名 狂気, 熱中
- **magic** 名 ①魔法, 手品 ②魔力
- **make a speech** 演説をする
- **make fun of** 〜を物笑いの種にする, からかう
- **make love** 愛の営みをする
- **make someone into a show** (人)をさらしものにさせる
- **make ~ into** 〜を…に仕立てる
- **Malcolm** 名 マルコム《人名》
- **manner** 名 ①方法, やり方 ②態度, 様子
- **many** 熟 so many 非常に多くの
- **Marcellus** 名 マーセラス《人名》
- **march off** 行進して去る
- **mark** 名 印, 記号, 跡
- **marriage** 名 結婚(生活・式)
- **married** 動 marry (結婚する)の過去, 過去分詞
- **marry** 動 結婚する
- **Mars** 名 マルス《ローマ神話》
- **meaning** 名 ①意味, 趣旨 ②重要性 double meaning 二重の意味
- **meanwhile** 副 それまでの間, 一方では
- **meek** 形 ①おとなしい, 従順な ②意気地のない Duncan the Meek 柔和王ダンカン
- **meeting** 名 ①集まり, ミーティング, 面会 ②競技会
- **memory** 名 記憶(力), 思い出
- **mention** 動 (〜について)述べる, 言及する
- **Mercury** 名 マーキュリー《ローマ神話》
- **mercy** 名 ①情け, 哀れみ, 慈悲 ②ありがたいこと, 幸運 beg for mercy 慈悲を請う
- **messenger** 名 使者, (伝言・小包などの)配達人, 伝達者
- **Michael Cassio** マイケル・キャシオ《人名》
- **middle** 名 中間, 最中 in the middle of 〜の真ん中[中ほど]に
- **midnight** 名 夜の12時, 真夜中, 暗黒
- **might** 助 《mayの過去》①〜かもしれない ②〜してもよい, 〜できる
- **mind** 名 ①心, 精神, 考え ②知性 lose one's mind 気が狂う
- **mirror** 名 鏡
- **miserable** 形 みじめな, 哀れな
- **mistaken** 形 誤った
- **mix** 動 ①混ざる, 混ぜる ②(〜を)一緒にする
- **moment** 名 ①瞬間, ちょっとの間 ②(特定の)時, 時期 at that moment その時に, その瞬間に for a moment 少しの間
- **monster** 名 怪物
- **Moor** 名 ムーア人
- **more** 熟 neither more nor less 超えることも下回ることもない no more もう〜ない no more than ただの〜にすぎない
- **mostly** 副 主として, 多くは, ほとんど
- **motion** 名 ①運動, 移動 ②身振り, 動作 put ~ into motion 〜を実行に移す
- **moving** 形 ①動いている ②感動させる
- **much** 熟 as much as 〜と同じだけ
- **murder** 名 人殺し, 殺害, 殺人事件 動 殺す
- **murderer** 名 殺人犯
- **my lord** 夫, 主人
- **mysterious** 形 神秘的な, 謎めいた

Word List

N

- **name** 熟 greet someone by name (人) の名前を呼びながら挨拶する
- **nature** 熟 human nature 人間性
- **near** 熟 drawing near 〜が近づいている
- **neither** 形 どちらの〜も…でない 代 (2者のうち) どちらも〜でない 副 《否定文に続いて》〜も…しない neither more nor less 超えることも下回ることもない neither 〜 nor … 〜も…もない
- **news** 名 報道, ニュース, 便り, 知らせ
- **newt** 名 イモリ
- **no longer** もはや〜でない [〜しない]
- **no more** もう〜ない no more than ただの〜にすぎない
- **no one** 誰も [一人も] 〜ない
- **nobility** 名 ①高貴さ ②《the −》貴族
- **noble** 形 気高い, 高貴な, りっぱな, 高貴な
- **nobleman** 名 貴族
- **nobly** 副 気高く
- **nonsense** 名 ばかげたこと, ナンセンス talk nonsense ばかなことを言う
- **nor** 接 〜もまたない neither more nor less 超えることも下回ることもない neither 〜 nor … 〜も…もない
- **not 〜 at all** 少しも [全然] 〜ない
- **not 〜 but …** 〜ではなくて…
- **not know if** 〜かどうかわからない
- **not so 〜 as …** …ほど〜でない
- **not yet** まだ〜してない
- **notice** 動 気づく, 認める
- **now** 熟 by now 今のところ, 今ごろまでには now that 今や〜だから, 〜からには

O

- **obedient** 形 従順な, 孝行な
- **obey** 動 服従する, (命令などに) 従う
- **occasionally** 副 時折, 時たま
- **of course** もちろん, 当然
- **off** 熟 be off to 〜へ出かける cut off 切断する, 切り離す march off 行進して去る
- **offend** 動 ①感情を害する ②罪を犯す, 反する
- **offer** 動 申し出る, 申し込む, 提供する
- **officer** 名 役人, 公務員, 警察官
- **one day** (過去の) ある日, (未来の) いつか
- **one-third** 3分の1
- **onto** 前 〜の上へ [に]
- **open grave** 墓穴
- **Ophelia** 名 オフィーリア《人名》
- **order** 熟 in order to 〜するために, 〜しようと
- **ordinary** 形 ①普通の, 通常の ②並の, 平凡な
- **organize** 動 組織する
- **Othello** 名 オセロー《人名》
- **otherwise** 副 さもないと, そうでなければ
- **out of** ①〜から外へ, 〜から抜け出して ②〜の範囲外に, 〜から離れて ③(ある数) の中から
- **owl** 名 フクロウ, ミミズク
- **own** 熟 of one's own 自分自身の

P

- **paid** 動 pay（払う）の過去, 過去分詞
- **palace** 名 宮殿, 大邸宅
- **pale** 形（顔色・人が）青ざめた, 青白い turn pale 青ざめる
- **participate** 動 参加する, 加わる
- **particular** 名 事項, 細部,《-s》詳細 in particular 特に, とりわけ
- **past** 形 過去の, この前の in times past 過去に 副 通り越して, 過ぎて
- **patient** 形 我慢［忍耐］強い, 根気のある
- **pay** 動 支払う, 払う, 報いる, 償う pay attention to ～に注意を払う
- **peace** 熟 at peace 平和に, 安らかに, 心穏やかで
- **perform** 動 ①（任務などを）行う, 果たす, 実行する ②演じる, 演奏する
- **perhaps** 副 たぶん, ことによると
- **permission** 名 許可, 免許
- **persuade** 動 説得する, 促して～させる
- **pirate** 名 海賊
- **pity** 名 哀れみ, 同情, 残念なこと
- **place** 熟 take the place of ～の代わりをする
- **plain** 形 簡素な
- **plainly** 副 はっきりと, 明らかに
- **plead** 動 ①嘆願する, 訴える ②弁護する, 弁解する
- **pleased** 形 喜んだ, 気に入った be pleased with ～が気に入る
- **pleasing** 形 心地のよい, 楽しい
- **pleasure** 名 喜び, 楽しみ, 満足, 娯楽
- **plot** 名 構想, 筋立て, プロット, 策略 動 構想を練る, たくらむ plot against ～に対抗して陰謀をたくらむ
- **point toward** ～の方角を指す
- **poison** 名 ①毒, 毒薬 ②害になるもの put poison into ～に毒を盛る 動 毒を盛る, 毒する
- **poisonous** 形 有毒な, 有害な
- **politeness** 名 丁寧さ, 慇懃
- **Polonius** 名 ポローニアス《人名》
- **popular with**《be -》～に人気がある
- **port** 名 港, 港町
- **position** 名 ①位置, 場所, 姿勢 ②地位, 身分, 職 ③立場, 状況
- **possible** 形 ①可能な ②ありうる, 起こりうる
- **posture** 名 ①姿勢 ②（気取った）態度
- **pour** 動 ①注ぐ, 浴びせる ②流れ出る, 流れ込む ③ざあざあ降る
- **poverty** 名 貧乏, 貧困, 欠乏, 不足
- **powerful** 形 力強い, 実力のある, 影響力のある
- **powerless** 形 力のない, 頼りない, 弱い
- **praise** 動 ほめる, 賞賛する
- **pray for** ～のために祈る
- **prayer** 名 ①祈り, 祈願（文）②祈る人
- **precious** 形 ①貴重な, 高価な ②かわいい, 大事な
- **predict** 動 予測［予想］する
- **prediction** 名 予言, 予報, 予測
- **prefer** 動（～のほうを）好む,（～のほうが）よいと思う
- **pretend** 動 ①ふりをする, 装う ②あえて～しようとする pretend to ～するふりをする
- **prettily** 副 きれいに, かわいらしく
- **Priam** 名 プライアム《人名》
- **prince** 名 王子, プリンス
- **prison** 名 ①刑務所, 監獄 ②監禁
- **private** 形 私的な, 個人の

WORD LIST

- **probably** 副 たぶん, あるいは
- **promise** 熟 keep one's promise 約束を守る
- **promote** 動 促進する, 昇進［昇級］させる
- **promotion** 名 昇進
- **proof** 名 証拠, 証明
- **proper** 形 ①適した, 適切な, 正しい ②固有の
- **proud** 形 ①自慢の, 誇った, 自尊心のある ②高慢な, 尊大な
- **prove** 動 ①証明する ②(〜であることが)わかる, (〜と)なる
- **pull 〜 apart** 〜を引き離す
- **punish** 動 罰する, ひどい目にあわせる
- **punishment** 名 ①罰, 処罰 ②罰を受けること
- **put in** 〜の中に入れる
- **put 〜 into ...** 〜を…に突っ込む
- **put 〜 into motion** 〜を実行に移す
- **put on** ①〜を身につける, 着る ②〜を…の上に置く
- **put poison into** 〜に毒を盛る
- **put to death** 処刑する

Q

- **quality** 名 ①質, 性質, 品質 ②特性 ③良質
- **queen** 名 女王, 王妃
- **quickly** 副 敏速に, 急いで
- **quietly** 副 ①静かに ②平穏に, 控えめに

R

- **rage** 名 激怒, 猛威, 熱狂
- **rang** 動 ring (鳴る) の過去
- **rash** 名 発疹, 吹き出物
- **rather** 副 ①むしろ, かえって ②かなり, いくぶん, やや ③それどころか逆に rather than 〜よりむしろ
- **react** 動 反応する, 対処する
- **reality** 名 現実, 実在, 真実(性)
- **realization** 名 ①理解, 認識 ②実現
- **realize** 動 理解する, 実現する
- **reason behind** 〜の背後にある理由
- **recently** 副 近ごろ, 最近
- **recognize** 動 認める, 認識［承認］する
- **recover** 動 ①取り戻す, ばん回する ②回復する
- **refuse** 動 拒絶する, 断る
- **Regan** 名 リーガン《人名》
- **regret** 動 後悔する, 残念ながら〜する 名 遺憾, 後悔, (〜に対する)悲しみ
- **relate** 動 ①関連がある, かかわる, うまく折り合う ②物語る be related to 〜と血縁関係にある
- **relief** 名 (苦痛・心配などの)除去, 軽減, 安心, 気晴らし
- **religion** 名 宗教, 〜教, 信条
- **reluctant** 形 気乗りしない, しぶしぶの be reluctant to 〜するのに気がすすまない
- **remain** 動 ①残っている, 残る ②(〜の)ままである［いる］
- **remarry** 動 再婚する
- **remind** 動 思い出させる, 気づかせる
- **reply** 動 答える, 返事をする, 応答する
- **reputation** 名 評判, 名声, 世評
- **request** 名 願い, 要求(物), 需要 動 求める, 申し込む

- **resemble** 動似ている
- **resist** 動抵抗[反抗・反撃]する, 耐える
- **respect** 名①尊敬, 尊重 ②注意, 考慮 動尊敬[尊重]する
- **respectful** 形礼儀正しい, ていねいな
- **responsible** 形責任のある, 信頼できる, 確実な
- **restore** 動元に戻す, 復活させる
- **revenge** 名復讐 take revenge on ～の恨みを晴らす 動復讐する
- **rid** 動取り除く get rid of ～を取り除く, 解雇する
- **right away** すぐに
- **rightful** 形正当な, 当然の
- **roof** 名屋根(のようなもの)
- **royal** 形王の, 女王の, 国立の
- **rude** 形粗野な, 無作法な, 失礼な
- **rudely** 副無礼に, 手荒く
- **rudeness** 名無礼, 礼儀知らず
- **ruin** 名破滅, 滅亡, 破産, 廃墟
- **rule over** 治める, ～を統治する
- **ruler** 名①支配者 ②定規
- **run away** 走り去る, 逃げ出す

S

- **sadly** 副悲しそうに, 不幸にも
- **sadness** 名悲しみ, 悲哀
- **sail** 名①帆, 帆船 ②帆走, 航海 set sail 出帆[出航]する 動①帆走する, 航海する, 出航する
- **sake** 名(～の)ため, 利益, 目的 for one's sake ～のために
- **satisfied** 形満足した
- **say to oneself** ひとり言を言う, 心に思う
- **scale** 名うろこ
- **scared** 形おびえた, びっくりした
- **scornful** 形軽蔑した, さげすむ
- **Scotland** 名スコットランド《英国の北部地方》
- **Scottish** 形スコットランド(人)の
- **sea voyage** 海洋航海
- **seal** 動～を封印する
- **secret** 形秘密の, 隠れた 名秘密, 神秘 keep ～ secret ～を秘密にする
- **secretly** 副秘密に, 内緒で
- **seduce** 動誘惑する, そそのかす, くどく
- **see ～ as ...** ～を…と考える
- **see if** ～かどうかを確かめる
- **seem** 動(～に)見える, (のように)思われる seem to be ～であるように思われる
- **selfish** 形わがままな, 自分本位の, 利己主義の
- **senator** 名上院議員, 元老院議員, (大学の)評議員
- **send away** 追い払う, 送り出す, ～を呼び寄せる
- **sense** 名①感覚, 感じ ②《-s》意識, 正気, 本性 ③常識, 分別, センス a sense of honor 廉恥心
- **serious** 形①まじめな, 真剣な ②重大な, 深刻な, (病気などが)重い
- **servant** 名召使, 使用人, しもべ
- **serve** 動①仕える, 奉仕する ②(客の)応対をする, 給仕する, 食事[飲み物]を出す
- **set sail** 出帆[出航]する
- **shaken** 動 shake(振る)の過去分詞
- **shame** 名①恥, 恥辱 ②恥ずべきこと, ひどいこと
- **shameful** 形恥ずべき, 下品な
- **shark** 名サメ(鮫)

WORD LIST

- **sharply** 副 鋭く, 激しく, はっきりと
- **shed** 動 (涙・血を)流す shed someone's blood (人)の血を流す
- **shelter** 動 避難する, 隠れる
- **shocked** 形 ～にショックを受けて, 憤慨して
- **shocking** 形 衝撃的な, ショッキングな
- **should have done** ～すべきだった(のにしなかった)《仮定法》
- **show** 熟 make someone into a show (人)をさらしものにさせる
- **shut** 動 ①閉まる, 閉める, 閉じる ②たたむ ③閉じ込める ④shutの過去, 過去分詞
- **sick** 熟 feel sick 気分が悪い
- **side** 名 側, 横, そば, 斜面
- **sight** 熟 at the sight of ～を見るとすぐに
- **silent** 形 ①無言の, 黙っている ②静かな, 音を立てない ③活動しない
- **silver** 形 銀(色)の
- **similarity** 名 類似(点), 相似
- **simply** 副 ①簡単に ②単に, ただ ③まったく, 完全に
- **sleeping** 形 眠っている, 休止している
- **slow to** 《be－》なかなか～しない
- **slowly** 副 遅く, ゆっくり
- **smother** 動 ①覆う, 包む ②窒息(死)させる, 息が詰まる
- **snake** 名 ヘビ
- **so** 熟 and so そこで, それだから, それで not so ～ as … …ほどでない so many 非常に多くの so that ～するために, それで, ～できるように so ～ that … 非常に～なので…
- **soak** 動 ①浸す, 浸る, ずぶぬれになる[する], しみ込ませる, しみ込む ②(浴びるように)酒を飲む soaked with ～でびしょぬれになる
- **soldier** 名 兵士, 兵卒
- **some** 熟 in some way 何とかして, 何らかの方法で
- **someday** 副 いつか, そのうち
- **somehow** 副 ①どうにかこうにか, ともかく, 何とかして ②どういうわけか
- **someone** 代 ある人, 誰か
- **something** 代 ①ある物, 何か ②いくぶん, 多少
- **sometimes** 副 時々, 時たま
- **soon** 熟 as soon as ～するとすぐ, ～するや否や
- **sorry** 熟 feel sorry for ～をかわいそうに思う
- **sort** 名 種類, 品質 a sort of ～のようなもの, 一種の～
- **soul** 名 ①魂 ②精神, 心
- **speech** 熟 make a speech 演説をする
- **speed** 名 速力, 速度
- **spirit** 名 ①霊 ②精神, 気力
- **spy** 動 ひそかに見張る, スパイする spy for ～のためにスパイする
- **stab** 動 ①(突き)刺す ②中傷する
- **stage** 名 ①舞台 ②段階
- **stare** 動 じっと[じろじろ]見る
- **stay in** 家にいる, (場所)に泊まる, 滞在する
- **stay with** ～の所に泊まる
- **steal** 動 ①盗む ②こっそりと手に入れる, こっそりと～する
- **sternly** 副 厳格に, 厳しく
- **steward** 名 ①給仕 ②スチュワード, 乗客係 ③執事, 世話係, 幹事
- **stir** 動 動かす, かき回す
- **stocks** 名 足かせ《軽微な罪を犯した人間を罰するための道具》
- **stole** 動 steal (盗む)の過去

113

- **storm** 名 嵐, 暴風雨
- **strangely** 副 奇妙に, 変に, 不思議なことに, 不慣れに
- **straw** 名 麦わら, ストロー
- **strawberry** 名 イチゴ
- **stream** 名 小川, 流れ
- **strength** 名 ①力, 体力 ②長所, 強み ③強さ, 濃度
- **strengthen** 動 高める, 強化する
- **stroke** 名 ①一撃, 一打ち ②一動作 ③一なで, 一さすり **stroke of thunder** 雷鳴
- **strongly** 副 強く, 頑丈に, 猛烈に, 熱心に
- **struggle** 動 もがく, 奮闘する **struggle with** 〜に苦悶する
- **stuck** 動 stick (刺さる) の過去, 過去分詞 **stuck in** 〜にはまり込んでいる
- **succeed** 動 ①成功する ②(〜の)跡を継ぐ
- **successful** 形 成功した, うまくいった
- **such a** そのような
- **such 〜 that ...** 非常に〜なので...
- **sudden** 形 突然の, 急な
- **suffer** 動 ①(苦痛・損害などを)受ける, こうむる ②(病気に)なる, 苦しむ, 悩む
- **suit** 名 ひとそろい, 一組
- **summon** 動 呼び出す, 要求する **summon courage to** 勇気を奮い起こして〜する
- **support** 動 ①支える, 支持する ②養う, 援助する
- **suppose** 動 ①仮定する, 推測する ②《be -d to 〜》〜することになっている, 〜するものである
- **surprised** 形 驚いた
- **surround** 動 囲む, 包囲する
- **survive** 動 ①生き残る, 存続する, なんとかなる ②長生きする, 切り抜ける
- **suspect** 動 疑う, (〜ではないかと)思う
- **suspected** 形 疑わしい
- **suspicion** 名 ①容疑, 疑い ②感づくこと
- **sweetly** 副 甘く, 優しく
- **sweet-tempered** 形 気の優しい
- **sword** 名 剣, 刀 **take out a sword** 剣を抜く
- **sword-fighter** 名 剣士
- **sympathetic** 形 同情する, 思いやりのある

T

- **take** 熟 **take away** ①連れ去る ②取り上げる, 奪い去る ③取り除く **take care of** 〜の世話をする, 〜を面倒を見る, 〜を管理する **take good care of** 〜を大事に扱う, 大切にする **take out** 取り出す, 取り外す, 連れ出す, 持って帰る **take over** 引き継ぐ, 支配する, 乗っ取る **take revenge on** 〜の恨みを晴らす **take the place of** 〜の代わりをする **take the throne** 王位に就く **take 〜 to ...** 〜を...に連れて行く
- **talk nonsense** ばかなことを言う
- **tell 〜 to ...** 〜に...するように言う
- **terrify** 動 脅かす, 恐れさせる
- **thane** 名 《昔のスコットランドの》豪族, 族長
- **thank 〜 for** 〜に対して礼を言う
- **thanks to** 〜のおかげで, 〜の結果
- **that** 熟 **so that** 〜するために, それで, 〜できるように **so 〜 that ...** 非常に〜なので... **such 〜 that ...** 非

WORD LIST

常に～なので…
- **then** 熟 from then on それ以来 just then そのとたんに
- **there lived** ～．～が住んでいた
- **therefore** 副 したがって, それゆえ, その結果
- **think fondly of** (人)のことを愛情を込めて考える
- **think of** ～のことを考える, ～を思いつく, 考え出す
- **though** 接 ①～にもかかわらず, ～だが ②たとえ～でも even though ～であるけれども, ～にもかかわらず 副 しかし
- **threat** 名 おどし, 脅迫
- **threaten** 動 脅かす, おびやかす, 脅迫する
- **throat** 名 のど, 気管 grab ～ by the throat ～の喉元をつかむ
- **throne** 名 王座, 王権 take the throne 王位に就く
- **throughout** 前 ①～中, ～を通じて ②～のいたるところに 副 初めから終わりまで, ずっと
- **thrown** 動 throw (投げる) の過去分詞
- **thrust** 動 強く押す, 押しつける, 突き刺す
- **thunder** 名 雷, 雷鳴 stroke of thunder 雷鳴
- **thus** 副 ①このように ②これだけ ③かくて, だから
- **time** 熟 at times 時には from that time on あれから, あの時以来 in times past 過去に over time 時間とともに, そのうち
- **tip** 名 先端, 頂点
- **tired** 形 ①疲れた, くたびれた ②あきた, うんざりした
- **title** 名 肩書, 称号
- **toad** 名 ヒキガエル
- **tongue** 名 舌

- **too** 熟 go too far 行き過ぎる, 度が過ぎる too well 十二分に
- **torture** 動 拷問にかける, ひどく苦しめる be tortured by ～に苦しむ [苛まれる]
- **tragedy** 名 悲劇, 惨劇
- **tragic** 形 悲劇の, 痛ましい
- **tragically** 副 悲惨に
- **traitor** 名 反逆者, 裏切り者
- **treat** 動 扱う treat someone badly (人)にひどい仕打ちをする
- **treatment** 名 取り扱い, 待遇
- **tremble** 動 震える, おののく
- **trick** 動 だます be tricked by ～にだまされる trick someone into だまして～させる
- **troublesome** 形 面倒な, やっかいな
- **Troy** 名 トロイ《国名》
- **true** 熟 come true 実現する
- **truly** 副 ①全く, 本当に, 真に ②心から, 誠実に
- **trust** 動 信用[信頼]する, 委託する 名 信用, 信頼, 委託
- **trusting** 形 (信じて) 人を疑わない
- **truth** 名 ①真理, 事実, 本当 ②誠実, 忠実さ
- **Turk** 名 トルコ人
- **Turkish** 形 トルコ(人・語)の 名 トルコ語
- **turn into** ～に変わる
- **turn pale** 青ざめる
- **turn to** ～の方を向く, ～に頼る, ～に変わる turn to leave その場を去ろうと振り返る
- **tyrant** 名 暴君, 専制君主

U

- **unable** 形《be – to ～》～すること

- □ **uncertain** 形 不確かな, 確信がない
- □ **underneath** 前 〜の下に, 〜真下に
- □ **understandable** 形 理解できる, わかる
- □ **unexpected** 形 思いがけない, 予期しない
- □ **unexpectedly** 副 思いがけなく, 突然に
- □ **unfaithful** 形 不誠実な
- □ **unfortunately** 副 不幸にも, 運悪く
- □ **ungrateful** 形 感謝しない, 恩知らずの
- □ **ungratefully** 副 恩知らずな態度で
- □ **unhappy** 形 不運な, 不幸な
- □ **unharmed** 形 無傷の
- □ **unkind** 形 不親切な, 意地の悪い
- □ **unkindly** 副 不親切に, 悪く
- □ **unkindness** 名 同情心の欠如
- □ **unkingly** 副 王らしからぬ
- □ **unlawful** 形 違法の, 不道徳な
- □ **unlike** 前 〜と違って
- □ **unnatural** 形 不自然な, 異常な
- □ **untrue** 形 真実でない, 事実に反する
- □ **unwisely** 副 愚かにも, 無分別に
- □ **up to** 〜まで, 〜に至るまで, 〜に匹敵して
- □ **upon** 前 ①《場所・接触》〜(の上)に ②《日・時》〜に ③《関係・従事》〜に関して, 〜について, 〜して
- □ **upset** 形 憤慨して, 動揺して **get upset** 取り乱す 動 気を悪くさせる, (心・神経など)をかき乱す

V

- □ **Venetian** 形 ヴェニスの
- □ **Venice** 名 ヴェニス《イタリアの都市》
- □ **victory** 名 勝利, 優勝
- □ **Viennese** 形 ウィーンの
- □ **virtue** 名 ①徳, 高潔 ②美点, 長所 ③効力, 効き目
- □ **vision** 名 ①視力 ②先見, 洞察力
- □ **voyage** 名 航海, 航行 **sea voyage** 海洋航海

W

- □ **wait for** 〜を待つ
- □ **wait impatiently** イライラして待つ
- □ **wake up** 起きる, 目を覚ます
- □ **walk around** 歩き回る, ぶらぶら歩く
- □ **wander** 動 ①さまよう, 放浪する, 横道にそれる ②放心する
- □ **warn** 動 警告する, 用心させる
- □ **warning** 名 警告, 警報
- □ **warship** 名 軍艦
- □ **way** 熟 **in any way** 決して, 多少なりとも **in every way** すべての点で **in some way** 何とかして, 何らかの方法で **in this way** このようにして **way of** 〜する方法 **way to** 〜する方法
- □ **weak** 熟 **grow weak** 弱る
- □ **wealth** 名 ①富, 財産 ②豊富, 多量
- □ **weapon** 名 武器, 兵器
- □ **wedding** 名 結婚式, 婚礼
- □ **wedding-sheets** 名 ウエディングシーツ
- □ **weed** 名 雑草
- □ **weep** 動 ①しくしく泣く, 嘆き悲

しむ ②しずくが垂れる
- **weird** 形 変わった, 妙な, 奇妙な
- **well** 熟 as well なお, その上, 同様に　as well as ～と同様に　too well 十二分に　well done うまくやった
- **well-respected** 形 とても尊敬されている
- **what if** もし～だったらどうなるだろうか
- **while** 熟 after a while しばらくして　for a while しばらくの間, 少しの間
- **whom** 代 ①誰を[に] ②《関係代名詞》～するところの人, そしてその人を
- **wicked** 形 悪い, 不道徳な
- **widow** 名 未亡人, やもめ
- **widowed** 形 夫と死別した
- **will have done** ～してしまっているだろう《未来完了形》
- **willow** 名 ヤナギ(柳)
- **win someone's heart** (人)のハートを射止める
- **wine** 名 ワイン, ぶどう酒
- **wing** 名 翼, 羽
- **wisdom** 名 知恵, 賢明(さ)
- **wise** 形 賢明な, 聡明な, 博学の
- **wisely** 副 賢明に
- **wish** 熟 I wish ～ were … 私が～なら …なのに。《仮定法過去》wish for 所望する
- **witch** 名 魔法使い, 魔女
- **within** 前 ①～の中[内]に, ～の内部に ②～以内で, ～を越えないで
- **woke** 動 wake(目が覚める)の過去
- **wolf** 名 オオカミ(狼)
- **womb** 名 子宮
- **wonder** 動 ①不思議に思う, (～に)驚く ②(～かしらと)思う　wonder about ～について知りたがる　wonder if ～ではないかと思う
- **work of** ～の仕業
- **worried** 形 心配そうな, 不安げな
- **worst** 形 《the –》最も悪い, いちばんひどい
- **worthless** 形 価値のない, 役立たずの
- **wound** 名 傷 動 負傷させる, (感情を)害する
- **wounded** 形 負傷した
- **write to** ～に手紙を書く
- **wrong** 熟 do wrong 罪を犯す
- **wrongdoing** 名 悪事, 不正行為

Y

- **yet** 熟 not yet まだ～してない

E-CAT

English **C**onversational **A**bility **T**est
国際英語会話能力検定

● E-CATとは…
英語が話せるようになるためのテストです。インターネットベースで、30分であなたの発話力をチェックします。

www.ecatexam.com

iTEP

● iTEP®とは…
世界各国の企業、政府機関、アメリカの大学300校以上が、英語能力判定テストとして採用。オンラインによる90分のテストで文法、リーディング、リスニング、ライティング、スピーキングの5技能をスコア化。iTEP®は、留学、就職、海外赴任などに必要な、世界に通用する英語力を総合的に評価する画期的なテストです。

www.itepexamjapan.com

ラダーシリーズ

Four Tragedies of Shakespeare
シェイクスピア四大悲劇

2015年11月8日 第1刷発行
2024年8月8日 第7刷発行

原著者　チャールズ・ラム
　　　　メアリー・ラム

発行者　賀川　洋

発行所　IBCパブリッシング株式会社
　　　　〒162-0804 東京都新宿区中里町29番3号
　　　　菱秀神楽坂ビル
　　　　Tel. 03-3513-4511　Fax. 03-3513-4512
　　　　www.ibcpub.co.jp

© IBC Publishing, Inc. 2010

印刷　株式会社シナノパブリッシングプレス
装丁　伊藤 理恵
組版データ　Arno Pro Regular+Goudy Old Style Regular

落丁本・乱丁本は、小社宛にお送りください。送料小社負担にてお取り替えいたします。
本書の無断複写（コピー）は著作権法上での例外を除き禁じられています。

Printed in Japan
ISBN 978-4-7946-0384-5

カバーイラスト　Tomoko Taguchi